Custom Fiori Applications in SAP HANA

Design, Develop, and Deploy Fiori Applications for the Enterprise

Sergio Guerrero

Apress®

Custom Fiori Applications in SAP HANA

Sergio Guerrero
Texas, TX, USA

ISBN-13 (pbk): 978-1-4842-6357-0   ISBN-13 (electronic): 978-1-4842-6358-7
https://doi.org/10.1007/978-1-4842-6358-7

Copyright © 2021 by Sergio Guerrero

Managing Director, Apress Media LLC: Welmoed Spahr
Acquisitions Editor: Divya Modi
Development Editor: Laura Berendson
Coordinating Editor: Divya Modi

Cover designed by eStudioCalamar

Cover image designed by Pixabay

Distributed to the book trade worldwide by Springer Science+Business Media New York, 1 New York Plaza, Suite 4600, New York, NY 10004-1562, USA. Phone 1-800-SPRINGER, fax (201) 348-4505, e-mail orders-ny@springer-sbm.com, or visit www.springeronline.com. Apress Media, LLC is a California LLC and the sole member (owner) is Springer Science + Business Media Finance Inc (SSBM Finance Inc). SSBM Finance Inc is a **Delaware** corporation.

For information on translations, please e-mail booktranslations@springernature.com; for reprint, paperback, or audio rights, please e-mail bookpermissions@springernature.com.

Apress titles may be purchased in bulk for academic, corporate, or promotional use. eBook versions and licenses are also available for most titles. For more information, reference our Print and eBook Bulk Sales web page at http://www.apress.com/bulk-sales.

Any source code or other supplementary material referenced by the author in this book is available to readers on GitHub via the book's product page, located at www.apress.com/ 978-1-4842-6357-0. For more detailed information, please visit http://www.apress.com/ source-code.

Printed on acid-free paper

*To my wife, Amy, for her unconditional support,
and to my children, Oliver and Emma*

To Tony and Ivette Villafranca

To the Guerrero and Jimenez families

Table of Contents

About the Author

Sergio Guerrero is a passionate software engineer with 10+ years of experience in web and database development in various technology stacks such as .NET and SAP HANA. He is the author of *Microservices on SAP HANA XSA* (Apress). On non-working days, Sergio cheers for the Green Bay Packers and Tigres UANL (MX soccer) or can be found grilling.

About the Technical Reviewer

Jose Ferez is an SAP ABAP Fiori consultant with more than 10 years of experience in different implementations and technologies and expertise in SAP Fiori, SCP, mobile services, and ABAP.

Jose worked as the main technical SAP Fiori reference for several implementations around the world, and has presented workshops and trainings since 2015.

Acknowledgments

I am thankful to my wife, Amy, and the people who are always there during the difficult times in my life. I am, again, very honored, humbled, and grateful for the Apress team and their valuable time: Divya, Laura, and Jose Ferez. Thank you for trusting me, and providing your guidance and different perspectives while I was writing this Fiori book. It has been a great journey and achievement.

Introduction

For many years, creating software applications in the SAP ecosystem was a headache; however, Fiori applications have changed the game when it comes to developing enterprise business applications that are simple to develop and meet complex rules across the enterprise. With their initial release over seven years ago and their fast adoption by many customers, Fiori applications are continuing to gain popularity due to Fiori's delightful UX and proven capabilities. Many customers focus on application integration, application and data security, ease of use, business adoption, and features that are offered by other modern, high-quality, and competitive frameworks. SAP Fiori stands tall among its peers and offers a world-class framework to create similar products. This book walks you through the journey of designing, collaborating, developing, testing, and deploying Fiori applications to on-premise and cloud environments. Various IDE tools are showcased to inform the reader of the many available ways to develop, extend, test, and enhance Fiori applications. By the end of the book, the reader will have been informed of all the phases, tools, and features and will have completed a sample Fiori application developed in the SAP Web IDE and deployed to the SAP HANA XSA environments on-premise and also to the AWS Cloud Platform.

Chapter 1 provides an explanation of what SAP Fiori applications are and it presents the five design principles for Fiori applications.

Chapters 2 and 3 relate to consuming data from a remote OData service and also mocking data when it is not available. The data models are consumed and presented in a Model View Controller (MVC) design pattern, which is a common pattern used in Fiori applications. External JavaScript libraries are integrated into the Fiori applications and presented in various devices to show its responsive features.

Chapter 4 shows and compares different unit testing frameworks used within the Fiori applications and also other open source frameworks, such as Nightmare and Puppeteer.

The book closes with Chapter 5 and the deployment of the sample Fiori application into an on-premise environment, and presents the steps to deploy the same application to the SAP Cloud Platform and also into Amazon Web Services.

All source code is available to readers on GitHub via the book's product page, located at www.apress.com/978-1-4842-6357-0. For more detailed information, please visit http://www.apress.com/source-code.

CHAPTER 1

Fiori Applications in SAP HANA

Welcome to building custom Fiori applications in SAP HANA. In this introductory chapter, I will explain what Fiori is, what concepts are important when starting the development of a product, why the initial design is very important, different design methodologies, understanding its current and future users, and how users will utilize the product during a process. Eventually a product moves from design into development and deployment. This book will conclude with a full exercise showcasing an entire Fiori application developed with all the concepts discussed throughout the book.

What Is Fiori?

Fiori refers to the User Experience (UX) design language created by SAP and adopted in their current and all future software products: for example, the Fiori Launchpad in S/4 HANA, the Fiori application library, the SAP HANA Cockpit for XSA, just to mention a few. An example is shown in Figure 1-1.

© Sergio Guerrero 2021
S. Guerrero, *Custom Fiori Applications in SAP HANA,*
https://doi.org/10.1007/978-1-4842-6358-7_1

Figure 1-1. *Sample SAP Fiori application*

SAP Fiori had its initial version in 2013; since then, three major versions have been released, and their themes are known as Gold Reflection (black & gold), Belize (blue), and Quartz (silver). The latest improved version, known as Fiori 3, was released in 2019, and it has the look and feel as shown in Figure 1-2.

Figure 1-2. *Fiori 3 UX*

The Fiori UX has also been extended to be included in mobile platforms such as IOS and Android for native devices. Developing applications for these devices requires additional programming languages, language runtimes, and simulators depending on the desired platform (as well as licensing if developing on the IOS platform). IOS devices use the SAP Fiori for IOS Guidelines and can be found here: `https://experience.sap.com/fiori-design-ios/`, while the Android devices use the SAP Fiori Guidelines for Android and can be found here: `https://help.sap.com/doc/c2d571df73104f72b9f1b73e06c5609a/Latest/en-US/docs/index.html`. Furthermore, there are hybrid applications that maintain the look and feel of the Fiori UX, and they are relevant due to the fact that they enhance and leverage the functionality provided by the mobile features.

Keep in mind that applications being built for IOS devices are required to be submitted to the app store for verification on the app store's specific rules, licensing, and other platform-dependent checks before they can be published. There are various types of IOS licenses that need to be considered if this is the desired end goal. Licenses for IOS apps can be found on the Apple developer website: `https://developer.apple.com/support/compare-memberships/`.

For the purpose of this book, only the web version of the SAP Fiori UX will be covered, and I point out the URLs for native development for the reader to learn where to find additional information related to specific mobile platform versions. Whether you are developing a Fiori application for web or mobile platforms, the following steps will be similar. Let's begin!

The first and foremost important step of any product is the **Design** step. It does not matter if the product is a consumer product, a software product, or any other type of product: all products should go through this step. I cannot emphasize this step enough – cutting corners during this step will result in additional work later.

Prior to creating a product, market research has to take place: Q&A sessions with possible users to see how the product will be utilized, how it can be beneficial for the users, and how to improve an initial prototype and eventually get as many details needed to help a company feel comfortable before starting to produce the product. The same concepts should also apply when creating a software product such as a Fiori application for the enterprise. Unfortunately, if you have been in the industry for a few years, you are probably familiar with some of the struggles that some development teams face when starting a new software application. If you noticed the last sentence, I went from analyzing a product, its users, and its potential uses to drastically showcasing a development team struggling, as is the situation in some companies. The reason I mentioned that is because it is a cruel reality that many teams face, and as developers working in the enterprise, we need to make sure we understand users' needs before starting any development efforts to minimize rework and increase software adoption in the long run. Software adoption is not easy, and it needs to be done carefully.

Fiori Design

As mentioned in the previous paragraph, design is a fundamental key component of the many steps to make a product succeed or fail. The more time invested upfront, the better prepared teams will be to develop products that will be adopted by users.

Design does not only imply that there has to be only a graphic designer prototyping, sketching, or performing any other type of drawing; designing means that there are design thinking sessions using Post-Its, whiteboard drawings, and whatever it takes to understand the use and/or flow of the product by its user(s). Do not attempt to solve a problem or try to come up with a solution at this point yet. This activity is strictly to understand a users' needs. (**Note** for developers) There will be enough time for solution solving later.

It is very important that during this step the entire team (technical and nontechnical resources) can participate. Using tools such as a plain **Whiteboard** can benefit the product team and the business as they can and should all participate in design ideas. With this approach, the design can easily be changed, and the design team should be able and open to receive constant feedback. This exercise may seem too simple sometimes; however, it is crucial for the contributors of any new product to gather ideas and quickly change things before committing to sketching or prototyping to understand the business need. This is shown in Figure 1-3.

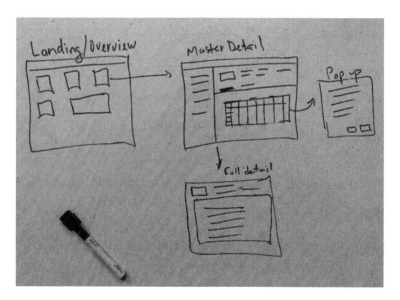

Figure 1-3. *Whiteboard design*

If the product team already has enough confidence in some of the design patterns for SAP Fiori, then they could proceed and move into sketching. There is one method called **Low-level design**, shown in Figure 1-4, which means that sketching can be achieved, and a designer usually mocks up what the screen high-level components will be (boxes, grids, lists, and other placeholders). Designers can also show application navigation from this type of design. Because it is simple enough and it gives the idea, it can be a quick gain for product teams. In the other hand, one of the drawbacks for this type of design method is that the customer may not fully understand the low-level design and they could become overwhelmed by not seeing the clear and wider picture of the prototype. Often, in our day and age where we have so many tools and applications that can be leveraged for this purpose, customers like to see what their product will look like. In my opinion the low-level design has a lesser adoption rate than the whiteboard or high-level design approach, which is discussed in the next paragraph.

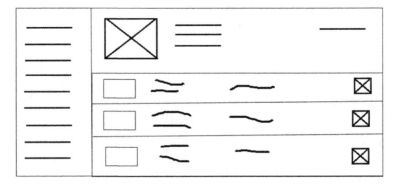

Figure 1-4. *Low-level design*

A third method of design is **High-level design**, and it is shown in Figure 1-5. This type of design means that a designer or a developer can start putting application controls (SAPUI5) on the screen and quickly build prototypes. Some RAD tools (Rapid Application Development) can be used for this purpose. This approach quickly shows the quicker application design to the customer. Most importantly, it shows exactly what the application will look like (not necessarily its behavior yet). Quite often customers wish to see exactly what they will receive at the end of development, and they assume that due to the prototype being done, then there is nothing else to do: wrong! Your team must let the customer know ahead of time about the prototype, and that development efforts are still needed on data integration, data binding, consuming data from web services, and moreover, adding any custom behavior such as business rules on the Fiori application.

Tools such as the SAP Web IDE (Integrated Development Environment), SAP Build (shown in Figure 1-6), and others can help you quickly complete high-level design prototypes using drag-and-drop features within these tools or WYSIWYG (**W**hat **Y**ou **S**ee **Is W**hat **Y**ou **G**et) editors.

Each of the tools mentioned here may require some license for production use. Please verify license requirements before using these tools.

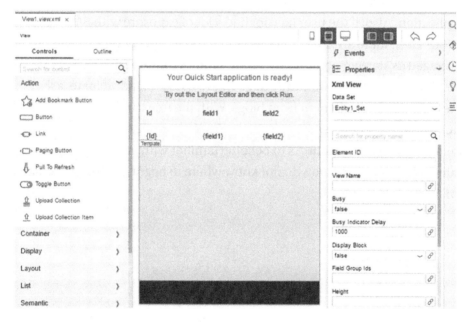

Figure 1-5. *SAP Web IDE layout editor*

If you decide to use the SAP Build tool, you will need to create an account and verify the license choices. The benefit of using the SAP Build tools is that you can prototype some of these applications, and including router navigation can also be achieved. SAP Build is simple enough to use even for nontechnical users. Many customers like the idea of having less technical dependency and having self-service tools; I think SAP Build could be a good tool for that purpose. There is a great feature within the SAP Build tool that allows the user to upload a spreadsheet to include data and immediately reflect it on the prototype that is being built. Once the prototype is close enough to what is needed, then it can be passed to the technical team to be integrated into the rest of the technical world.

With the paid license of the SAP Build tool, a user may create multiple projects and keep them in their account. These prototypes/projects can then be imported into the SAP Web IDE where a web developer can continue their work by adding JavaScript code to the rest of the application. Also, if the user has not had a lot of exposure with SAP Build or SAP Fiori, there are some templates in the Gallery section that can be leveraged as starting points of someone's prototyping learnings. There are also blogs, and a community page where users can participate, ask questions, and even benefit from blogs. With the free trial license in SAP Build, designers/developers can only create one application project. There are plenty of online resources to become familiar with and join in these online communities. If you do not know where to begin, explore within the SAP Build community.

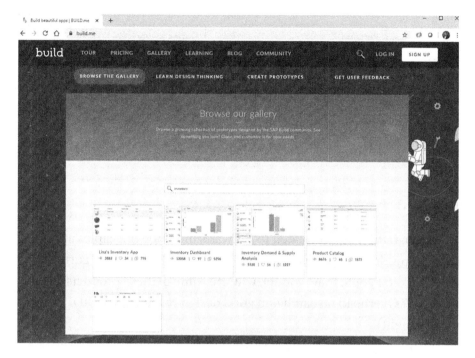

Figure 1-6. *SAP Build tool*

Whether the design is done with a whiteboard or a low- or high-level design, the end goal of this step is to understand users and how they will interact with a product; therefore, your team needs to focus on such a goal. It is beneficial to include targeted audience users and create a fictitious persona.

A **persona** identifies an ideal fictitious user, their working environment, their gender, their tasks, how they will use the product, and any external factors, impediments, possible restrictions, or other metadata about this user in relationship to their interaction with a product (in our case it is software) as shown in Figure 1-7. In addition to understanding the user needs, there also must be some research about any pain points that are currently encountered by the user community and how this new product can minimize, or even better, eliminate them. The goals for a Fiori design are to make the best and most efficient product that users are glad to have and that they will enjoy using to accomplish their day-to-day tasks.

9

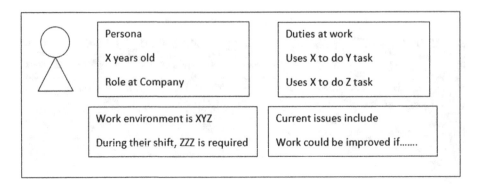

Figure 1-7. Persona

Although this book is related to software, the same principles apply to any other products, so let us analyze some successful products currently in the market. People may wonder, why are some of these products so successful? Overhead research and good design result in great ROI (return on investment).

One product brand I would like to analyze is one that builds power tools, construction tools, and tool storage, just to mention a few. These tools are of very high quality and they can last for a very long time. These tools are the choice of most construction professionals. They are on the higher end of products of their industry. When I got married over a decade ago, I acquired different types of tools for home improvement projects. My first set of tools was great when I started learning how to do some of the smaller home projects. As I have gained experience and learned more about tool quality, I have noticed that the right tool will get the job done correctly. Yes, I could have had a cheaper tool, but it is not the same as using the correct tool. I started investing in more of these black and yellow tools. The latest toolkit I got was a set of drills and impact drills with a battery charger and two batteries. Compared to my older tools and throughout the years, the new tools have gotten lighter, they have more power than before, the battery life has been improved, and some of different tools can share batteries. In my opinion, this company has done extensive UX research, tool design, and a vast number of improvements on their tools, resulting in customer satisfaction, increasing product adoption, and returning customers; all of this is what most companies want to see. All these satisfactory measures resulted in great ROI for this company. I do not mind spending a few extra dollars to be able to get a good-quality tool. As you can read in this paragraph, there were possible personas (construction professionals), customer research as to how customers use these tools, and identifying some of the pain points for these users such as tool weight, battery life, and compatibility of tool parts between tools. All these concepts are part of the design to development and production of a product. Such a process is also recommended by SAP; it is known as design thinking and it is a proven process that spans throughout the life cycle of creating a product. The design thinking process starts in the discovery phase, where things are presented and analyzed, and many notes are taken when creating a product; the design phase includes various methods of presenting and prototyping an idea to see how it will be used and observed by many collaborators in the team with the purpose of providing feedback and capture how users will use this product: basically all hands on board. Develop is the part in which the people create the product, present it to their customer counterpart for feedback, and enhance it during several iterations; and finally Deliver, which is the rewarding part of the process when the product leaves the team and is put into productive use.

Five Design Principles of Fiori

The Fiori UX has five design principles that must apply to all applications, and they are shown in Figure 1-8:

1) Role-based

2) Coherent

3) Simple

4) Responsive

5) Delightful

SAP Fiori UX Design Principles

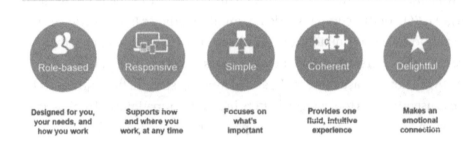

Figure 1-8. *Five Fiori design principles*

Role-based is an equally important feature as the other ones in the design principle; however, in my opinion it is the most important one, as it seems to be the one that most customers really ask for. The role-based feature can set control properties to read-only, enable/disable visibility, or allow users to be able to provide inputs. Another role-based use case of Fiori applications is for users from different departments within a company to be able to see different parts of an application; for example, Human Resource users will have a different view of the same app than a user from Accounting than a user from another department. Further, these roles can be compared to roles from Active Directory on non-Fiori applications. When designing Fiori applications, you may think of this property as a way to show the same application for a user who has read and write access vs. a different user who can only read some data and cannot interact with it. If you can imagine read-only vs. read and write, then you are thinking about the role-based feature. When the Fiori applications are added into the SAP Fiori Launchpad, roles can also allow or prevent users from accessing Fiori applications. In this book, we will not go into the Launchpad configuration; instead, we will deploy our Fiori application into an SAP HANA XSA environment in chapter 5.

Coherent is the part of the design principle that forces the design of the application to make sense in every aspect that it does and how it behaves. In old SAP R/3, some transactions required so many input parameters that sometimes the user did not understand why the app required them; sometimes, the users even needed to click an element to show additional information. Moreover, the coherent principle results in additional process improvements when designing new software for these business scenarios. This feature can be thought of as a wizard or a smart table with default filters shown in the smart filter bar or when using the type property in a button to show accept (displayed in green), reject (displayed in red), or default (default color). Other UI5 controls may use the state property to show other statuses, such as warnings, enabled, or disabled, just to mention a few.

Simple is one of my favorite features because as developers in the SAP world, some SAP transactions are very complex and they require many fields to be provided even if we did not know what those fields were supposed to be used for. The simple feature here refers to minimizing the number of clicks, keeping the user more productive, and making their process as efficient as possible. The maximum number of clicks to be included within a process or transaction to allow the user to accomplish a task is supposed to be less than three.

Responsive means that traditional software had to be written for different platforms; however, SAP Fiori leverages the responsiveness feature of its software to be able to write a single code base and be able to adapt this software on different screen sizes and devices with little to no additional effort from the technical point of view. The responsive feature of Fiori applications immediately reflects ROI for companies, as they can develop these applications for the office environment or the manufacturing floor at the same time. The very good responsive applications will also be able to run in a mobile browser allowing users to be informed about their business on the go as shown in Figure 1-2. The SAP Web IDE and the SAP Build tool have "Device Preview" features where you can immediately see how the design will look in different devices.

Delightful means that if the user likes it, chances are they will be coming back to do their work or to use their application. It is more likely to be productive and keep users happy with good-looking applications, and that is why it is so important to include this principle. Customer adoption of software is a very difficult task to achieve when designing and developing new software. Users will complain and say that the current system works, even if it is inefficient, and they will resist change. From prior experience in other platforms where there is too much freedom on design and development, it is also more tedious and complex not having this part of the framework.

The five Fiori principles can be visualized from a comparison of the Figures 1-9 and 1-10. Figure 1-9 showcases the SAP GUI transaction, and Figure 1-10 displays a Fiori application with an Object page and an icon tab bar.

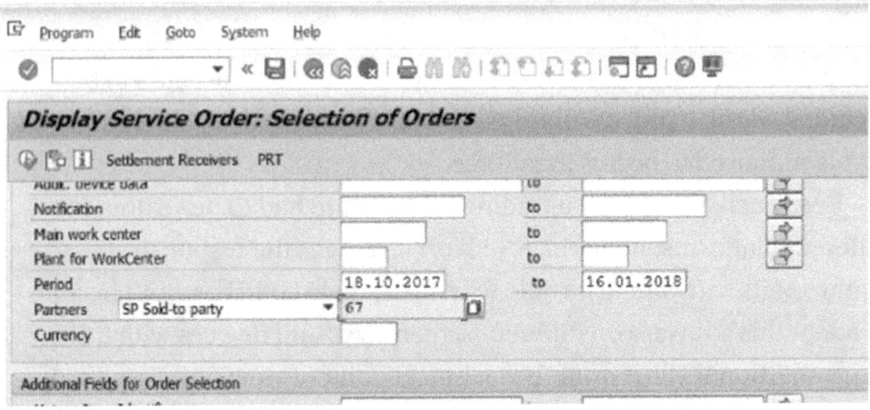

Figure 1-9. *SAP GUI*

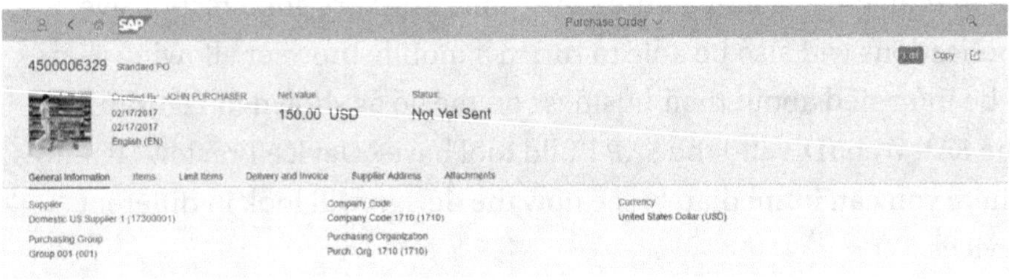

Figure 1-10. *SAP Fiori standard application*

Getting Your System Ready for Fiori Applications

While all the explanations to understand Fiori design, UX, and all the initial concepts to create a great product are necessary, your developer side may be wondering when to get into the system and start prototyping and developing some of these Fiori applications.

Fiori provides a set of stencils to get you ready for the world of Fiori applications. These stencils are found at https://experience.sap.com/fiori-design-web/downloads/#top. These stencils contain templates, controls, colors, fonts, icons, and everything you will need to get started with your design. There are stencils and programs for Mac and Windows-based users. I will not get too deep into the design aspect as I am more familiar with the development side of the house. When the design is completed, then those mockups and other deliverables from the design team can be passed to a developer to start their development.

There are various tools to develop the Fiori application. Tools such as the SAP Web IDE (found on SAP Cloud Platform, on premise, or in the Web IDE personal edition) shown in Figure 1-11 and the Business Application Studio are used for this type of Fiori development.

Figure 1-11. *SAP Web IDE*

The Business Application Studio is the newest tool for Fiori and HANA development and is a set of plug-ins for Visual Studio IDE (it can also be found on the SAP Cloud Platform: look under the Cloud Foundry Platform ➤ Subscriptions ➤ SAP Business Application Studio and then click subscribe), and it is shown in Figure 1-12. If you are not able to access it, then check that your user has the *Business Application Studio Developer* role template.

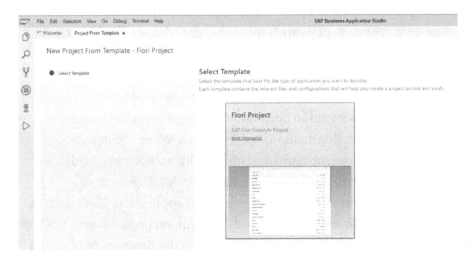

Figure 1-12. *SAP Business Application Studio*

There are also some SAP Fiori plug-ins available for SAP Fiori if you decide to use Visual Studio Code IDE.

These plug-ins are found in the extensions as shown in Figure 1-13.

Figure 1-13. *SAP Fiori plug-in for Visual Studio Code*

Since I have introduced the tools for development, now it is important to know how to start the development for your custom Fiori application.

Fiori applications are built on top of the **SAPUI5** JavaScript library. The SAPUI5 JS library is a set of HTML5 controls and CSS3 styles built by SAP for the purpose of creating Fiori applications. All SAP consumers with a paid license can get access to create these SAPUI5 / Fiori applications. On the other hand, if you are not an SAP customer and would like to build some SAP like Fiori applications using UI5, there is an open source version called OpenUI5. Some differences of these two libraries are highlighted in Table 1-1.

Table 1-1. *Comparison between SAPUI5 and OpenSAPUI5*

	SAPUI5	**OpenUI5**
Library type	Available for SAP customers	Open source library
License type	SAP	Apache 2.0
Runs on	SAP HANA, SAP Cloud Platform or SAP NetWeaver front-end server	Any web server
Website	`https://sapui5.hana.ondemand.com/`	`https://openui5.org/`
Application types	SAP front-end server • SAP Fiori apps • SAP Fiori freestyle apps SAP HANA eXtended Application Services (XS engine) • Custom Fiori apps	Any web application or web component
Developed by	SAP	SAP and open source community

In addition to the preceding table comparison, let us take a moment to understand the SAPUI5 SDK (Software Development Kit) page, as I will highlight important content and what readers trying to get into SAPUI5 / Fiori development should be aware of.

In Figures 1-14 and 1-15, we can observe the SAPUI5 SDK and the OpenUI5 SDK pages, respectively. They both have similar look and feel as well as the same structure; again, these different libraries are used for either SAP licensed development or for the open source equivalent of the UI5 framework.

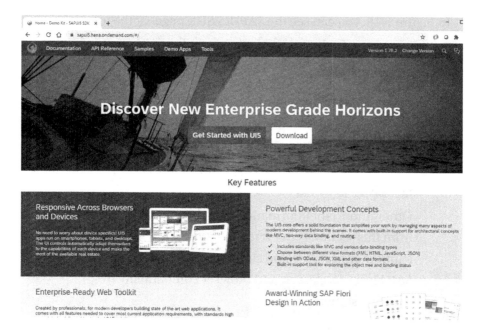

Figure 1-14. *SAPUI5 SDK*

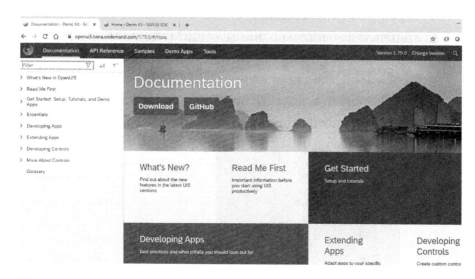

Figure 1-15. *Open UI5 SDK*

In Figure 1-16, you can see the SAPUI5 SDK page. At the top of the page, there are some sections (tabs) into which the content is divided.

1) **Documentation**

In this section, the reader can find all the important documentation related to SAPUI5 applications from walkthrough to create their first Fiori application, to understanding the deep concepts of Fiori applications.

Other important information valuable to remember from this section is the version features, the version support, how to develop custom controls, themes, SAP Fiori CSS classes, and browser compatibility to mention some.

Spending time in the Walkthrough section is extremely important as it shows how to build a Fiori application from beginning to end. It also shows different scenarios with the use of the MVC (Model View Controller) pattern. Whether you are building a new application or extending an SAP-delivered application, this section of the SDK is useful, and it is recommended to become familiar with it.

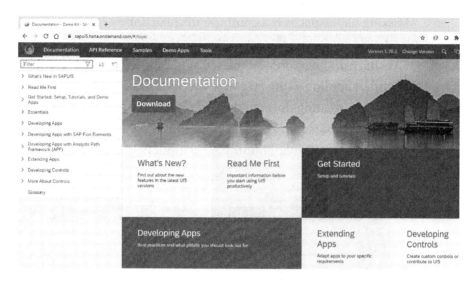

Figure 1-16. *SAPUI5 SDK documentation page*

2) **API Reference**

The API reference is very helpful since all the
SAPUI5 controls are explained: the controls are
broken down into properties, events, constructors,
associations, aggregations, and their cardinality.
This is shown in Figure 1-17.

In this SAPUI5 SDK section, the developer can
obtain a full understanding of all the necessary
attributes, inheritance, and behavior of each
control. Furthermore, this section breaks down the
SAPUI5 controls based on the namespace (sap.m,
sap.apf, sap.ui, sap.f…).

When you decide to start building your Fiori
applications and it requires controls from
different namespaces in your XML views, make
sure to include references to those namespaces.

Missing namespaces is a common mistake done by developers when they start their venture in SAPUI5. Another common missed step is the lack of understanding of the available properties; spend some time reading through the API reference and familiarize yourself with some of the common controls such as tables, buttons, and input fields.

Figure 1-17. *SAPUI5 SDK API reference*

3) **Samples**

Yes, the SDK page provides sample application and code snippets that a developer can quickly see on the user interface, as shown in Figure 1-18. As a developer learns more and more, some of the code snippets will be easy to remember, but it is still very helpful to know where to get these controls in case a new control is required when developing a new application. The important sections within this tab are

a) The control navigation list shown on the left side of the application

b) The number of different scenarios shown in the list item

c) The version of the SAPUI5 library being used (top right-hand side of the screen)

d) Code snippet icon shown as a { = } right under the Change version and the magnifying glass icon on the top right-hand corner of Figure 1-18

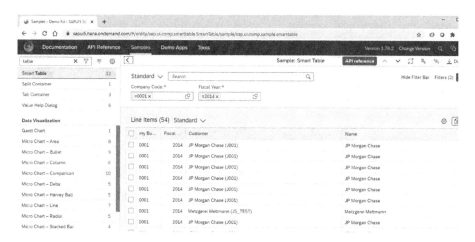

Figure 1-18. *SAPUI5 SDK sample page*

4) **Demo Apps**

SAP has provided some demo apps as shown in Figure 1-19 so that developers can see what has been done, and how it was done, and if they need to, they get the code base in case their requirement is similar to the demo applications. I would like to highly recommend visiting and going over the Walkthrough application first to get a full understanding of all the moving pieces that exist in

an SAP Fiori application. If you are able to follow
this application and understand how the many
pieces coordinate and work with each other, then
it will be very easy to understand any other Fiori
application whether you will be modifying an
existing one or creating new from scratch.

Make sure to spend enough time in this demo app
section, especially in the *Walkthrough* as shown in
Figure 1-19.

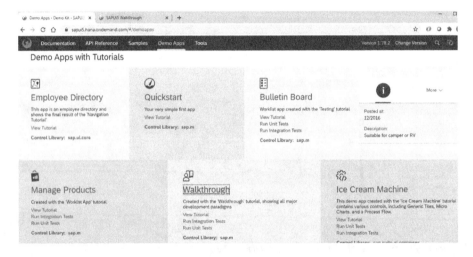

Figure 1-19. *SAPUI5 SDK demo apps*

5) **Tools**

This section points out the main tools required
to build SAP Fiori applications, as shown in
Figure 1-20. These tools are used for development
(SAP Web IDE or UI5 tooling), debugging (UI5
inspector), theme designer (in case you need a
custom theme), and icons. Additional description
of these tools is found next.

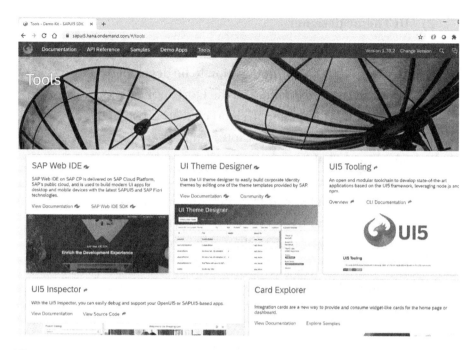

Figure 1-20. *SAPUI5 SDK tools page*

In Figure 1-20, you can see the description of the main tools and a link to learn more about them.

1) **SAP Web IDE**

This is the main development tool for SAP Fiori applications. It is a browser-based tool used to develop web and database applications. There are several versions of this type of tool, so please check out the required version and license requirements for your development. The SAP Web IDE can be installed locally (SAP Web IDE personal edition), there is a version on the SAP Cloud Platform called SAP Web IDE Full stack, and there is also a version for on-premise development which can also be accessed from the SAP HANA Express edition.

25

2) **UI Theme designer**

This tool, shown in Figure 1-21, is recommended to be used if the SAPUI5 application to be developed requires a custom theme and the Fiori application will not follow the standard Fiori concepts. Look inside this tool in the SAP Cloud Platform (or SAP Cloud Platform trial edition) and see if you can come up with your own custom-branded theme. This tool is extremely helpful as it allows the developer to reuse the class names and the developer may be able to change the colors dynamically and quickly see what their application may look like if the custom theme was utilized as the end product.

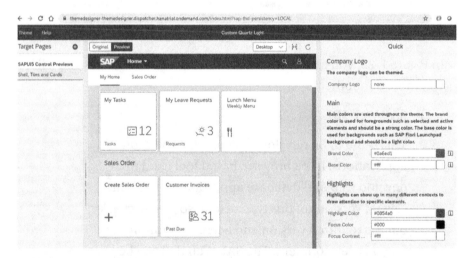

Figure 1-21. *SAP Cloud Platform custom theme designer*

3) **UI5 Tooling**

This is a command-line interface (CLI) tool, shown in Figure 1-22, that allows quicker development of applications leveraging Node JS and NPM (Node Package Manager). CLI tools have gained a lot of popularity in web development and it is no surprise that this is available in SAPUI5.

Figure 1-22. *UI5 tooling CLI*

4) **UI5 Inspector**

This tool is a Chrome browser add-on tool that allows developers to debug and analyze SAPUI5 controls on their application when it is running on the browser. This tool is shown in Figure 1-23. This tool displays the hierarchical representation of a control within the application as well as all the css classes and any other attribute/property assigned to it. This tool is helpful when trying to debug a specific control behavior or look within an application. Since different browsers behave and display differently, this tool may be used in cases when comparing different browser behaviors while comparing certain controls and how they render on the screen.

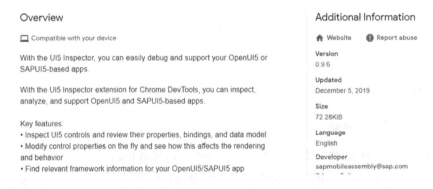

Overview

🖳 Compatible with your device

With the UI5 Inspector, you can easily debug and support your OpenUI5 or SAPUI5-based apps.

With the UI5 Inspector extension for Chrome DevTools, you can inspect, analyze, and support OpenUI5 and SAPUI5-based apps.

Key features:
• Inspect UI5 controls and review their properties, bindings, and data model
• Modify control properties on the fly and see how this affects the rendering and behavior
• Find relevant framework information for your OpenUI5/SAPUI5 app

Additional Information

🏠 Website   ❗ Report abuse

Version
0.9.6

Updated
December 5, 2019

Size
72.28KiB

Language
English

Developer
sapmobileassembly@sap.com

***Figure 1-23.** SAPUI5 inspector*

5) **Icon explorer**

By far this is my favorite tool, as it allows me to
find available icons within the same framework.
Sometimes, in other technology frameworks,
developers need to integrate additional js libraries
for icons, while in SAPUI5, the icon library is already
included. This tool allows a developer to search
for icons and the icons can be presented in various
forms such as different icon sizes. Moreover, the
icons are tagged with some keywords to easily find
them while searching them in this tool as shown in
Figure 1-24.

Figure 1-24. *SAPUI5 icon explorer*

Understanding Elements, Layouts, and Floor Plans

As we dive deeper and deeper into Fiori, it is important to understand how
Fiori applications are designed and developed. If you have not developed
a Fiori application before, most likely you are going to see examples and
try to mimic them. This is a normal process when learning a new skill or
technology or when trying something new for the first time. Experienced

developers also look for patterns and components that make up a type of application. We try to understand what elements make up a page and what controls are used and become familiar with them via some API or documentation. This is also the case when developing Fiori applications.

SAPUI5 controls include the most common controls in web applications, such as input fields, labels, combo boxes, tables, and check boxes, among many others. Please visit the SAPUI5 SDK page to learn more about the different types of controls, their documentation, and their code samples.

SAP Fiori **Elements**, formerly known as Smart templates, provide you with the most common set of templates that are used in Fiori applications. Some of these templates include the Overview page, the List Report, the Worklist, and the Object page. Moreover, some of these Fiori elements require little to no development, and they are metadata-driven applications. This book will show the use of creating these applications using the MVC framework, XML views, and the JavaScript programming language in controllers.

1) **Overview:** This template contains smart tiles that may have some important metrics such as analytical cards, allowing a user to quickly see and navigate to see more details. The purpose of an Overview page is as the name describes, to provide a quick view of important information without the need to drill down into every area/page of an application to find out an issue with the system. This type of page/template is used as an entry point of an application, as shown in Figure 1-25. This template showcases cards, tiles, lists, and some graphs for quick visuals. A picture is worth a thousand words and this type of template does exactly that. It does not overwhelm the user and it provides a clear idea of what to look for.

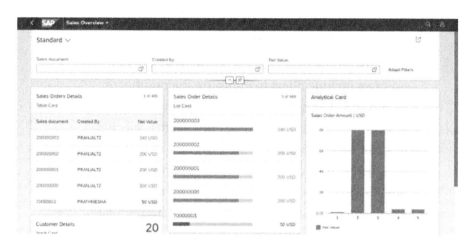

Figure 1-25. *Overview template*

2) **Worklist:** This type of page/template is used for
    assigning work to a user, and often it lets the user
    drill down into details to take some action. It is a
    simple list to detail page. This template showcases
    a list, a navigation, and a detail page where item
    details can be seen and acted upon. Figure 1-26
    shows such a template.

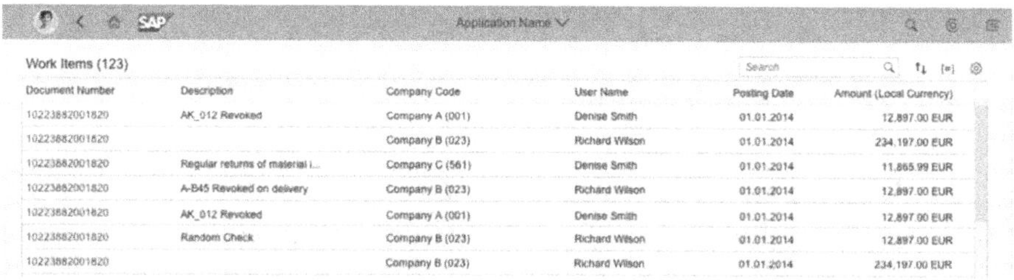

Figure 1-26. *Worklist template*

3) **List Report:** This type of template is very similar to the Worklist template; however, this template is often used for a larger data set of items where the user can include filters to minimize the number of records displayed. The template also allows multiple selection to perform a set of actions against specific records, and it is normally used to give a higher-level visibility of the data set to the user in comparison to the Worklist, which is normally used for a smaller set of data dedicated to a specific user. This template can be seen in Figure 1-27.

Figure 1-27. *List Report template*

4) **Object page:** This template is used to provide details about a specific record. It is used as the detailed step where navigation from a list item is clicked and navigated to here. This template is used to provide concrete details about a record. This template is composed of header-level data attributes such as object header, number, image of the object, title, status, and object attributes.

This template can also contain tabs to separate and logically display data related to specific subcategories related to the item in context. Some of the Fiori apps use this type of template when needing to provide an extensive detail view of a record. This template can be seen in Figure 1-28.

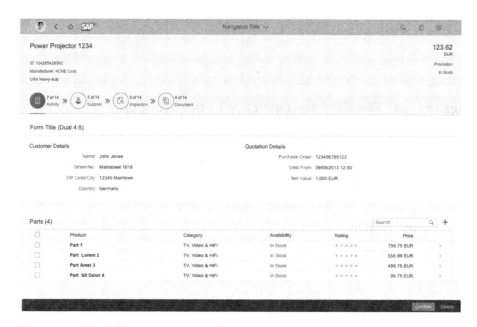

Figure 1-28. *Object view template*

Layouts at a high level are placeholders for the developers to place content on the screen. There are various types of layouts: for example, dynamic layout for the full screen as shown in Figure 1-29, the flexible column layout with two or three columns as shown in Figure 1-30.

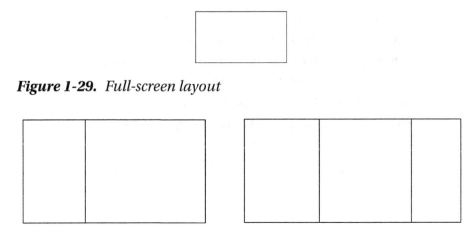

Figure 1-29. *Full-screen layout*

Figure 1-30. *Flexible layout with two or three columns*

Floor plans refer to how the elements can be placed inside the layouts to be able to create a more complete application. Depending on the layout selection, there may be one or more floor plans that could be added inside the layouts. The full-screen layout can have one type of element, for example the Worklist.

The flexible column layout is usually made up of a master/detail template, in which the **Master (UI)** view contains a list that is used for navigation, while the detail side of the template shows the details related to the selected item from the **(UI)** view. Very similar to the flexible column layout of two columns, the layout with three columns is often used for a master-detail-detail scenario. The reason to have some of these two- and three-column layouts is to avoid multiple navigations of the app keeping the user focused on the same screen while presenting related information on the various layouts.

It is important to highlight **Smart controls** as part of the components used within the Fiori applications. Smart controls are those that are created from when an OData service is present in the Fiori application and the metadata of this service is used to build Smart controls. The Smart controls include smart filters, control configuration to include visible fields, and export to Excel, just to mention a few of the features, as shown in Figure 1-18 as well. The smart filter bar can generate the smart input field controls and provides application filtering capability without the need to code a single line of code. It is managed entirely by the framework. Should your application require custom filtering or additional enhancements to the smart filter bar, then it is possible to leverage the functionality provided and include the custom handlers ourselves as custom extensions to the code. Most of the configurations for these Smart controls is done when placing the controls in the XML view and include the control attributes that are eventually bound to an OData service.

OData services are fundamental in Fiori applications, as these services are used to expose or consume data from web clients via HTTP(s). OData is a protocol that has a very heavy use in Fiori applications as well as in other web technologies. SAP Fiori (UI5) controls primarily use two different versions of OData, v2 and v4. OData returns data in atom XML and in JSON formatted data. OData services can be queried based on the OData syntax rules as documented in the OData protocol. When creating some Fiori applications, there are also wizards to include an OData endpoint (URL), and the wizard includes the OData model and the metadata file and prepares the application to consume this type of service. OData will be discussed in depth in Chapter 2.

Conclusion

As we conclude our initial chapter, I hope you can understand the reasons that Fiori design is an important task prior to commencing any development of an application and is a fundamental pillar to the success of a software product development.

Spending more time when initially designing a product will reduce unnecessary iterations between development teams and product owners or customers. Greater effort spent at the beginning of your project will allow the product to be more successful and increase its ROI. A second learning point within the first chapter is to become familiar with the SAP Fiori principles and SAP Fiori concepts such as components, elements, layouts, and floor plans in order to suggest them to clients and apply them when designing and developing SAP Fiori applications. Finally, understanding the integration points between SAP Fiori applications and what to expect from certain technologies involved will be fundamental to prepare your teams for a fun and exciting adventure. Familiarize yourself with various development tools, compare them, and choose the right ones, so you know when to use each of them for your scenarios. Thank you for completing this chapter and without further delay get ready to jump into the next chapter, where we will dive deep into the OData protocol and RESTful APIs.

CHAPTER 2

Consuming Data in Fiori Applications

Welcome to Chapter 2! This chapter will explain all about data and data models. You will learn how to consume data, how to mock data when it is not present, how to simulate data from a local JSON model, and how to expose data. Consuming data models via OData (Open Data protocol created by Microsoft and adopted by others) and JSON (JavaScript Object Notation) models are key concepts in SAP Fiori. Sometimes, it is necessary to consume external REST API (**Re**presentational **S**tate **T**ransfer) services from your SAP Fiori application. This chapter will touch on all these points from the SAP Fiori application point of view and also from a unit testing tool called POSTMAN REST client, which can be used in parallel while developing your front-end application, but you may not be ready to implement all of the XML views and JavaScript code necessary to make the data integration. Get ready to jump into technical concepts and let us learn together.

Understanding Data and Mocking It When Not Available

In Chapter 1, the book described various ways to design your applications using different tools and collaborating with key users to create a successful design. Within the design step, sometimes users provide data samples

© Sergio Guerrero 2021
S. Guerrero, *Custom Fiori Applications in SAP HANA*,
https://doi.org/10.1007/978-1-4842-6358-7_2

using spreadsheets to be used within the design so that designers and developers can visualize when they need to represent as a list of data, a single entry of data, or data being inputted from a screen via user interaction. In this chapter, the book is gradually moving from the design concept into being able to understand data a little better. Understanding data is very important, as it applies to a back-end database system and also while creating front-end applications so that they can be performant and able to present only relevant data within the application/product being developed. Understanding data is a key component while designing and while creating an application.

Developers sometimes wonder how they should start developing an application if data is not available from a back-end system. Sometimes developers start their work simulating data as hard-coded JSON objects in their application. Luckily for most enterprise projects, data usually comes from an ERP (Enterprise Resource Planning) system and there is plenty of data available to be consumed. Data models in these systems are usually created as CDS (Core Data Services views) if they come from SAP or SAP HANA and are exposed as OData service endpoints that are easily consumed from a REST client or application.

CDS is a scripted language created by SAP that allows developers to create design-time objects such as entities (tables) and data models (views) with the purpose of doing most of the work closer to the database. CDS views may contain additional annotations that are leveraged by UI5 controls to achieve less coding in the front end and these data annotations are controlled from the back end. Even if data is nonexistent in the back-end system table, but the data model is created, the OData service generates a metadata file that provides information about the endpoint, where the data model is exposed, the data types for the different data entities are known, and further, the OData service sometimes can contain data annotations that are used by applications.

Let me break down the previous paragraph into smaller chunks:

1) **OData**

   This is the (open data) protocol/technology that generates an OData service that can be easily consumed by web applications or other REST clients. OData has a huge adoption in SAP Fiori. It is the main and preferred way to expose and consume data in SAP Fiori applications. It is also present in other technology stacks. OData APIs, also known as OData services, have been released in different versions. The most common version is OData v2. The latest version of OData services is OData v4.

   These two versions have the following similarities and differences. Most of the SAPUI5 controls that are used in Fiori applications use OData v2. In Table 2-1 we can see this comparison.

Table 2-1. *OData V2 vs OData V4 comparison*

OData V2	OData V4
Microsoft Open Specification Promise (OPS)	Approved by OASIS and ISO
Data exposed as atom/XML (default) or JSON	Data exposed as JSON (default) XML is optional
	DateTime data type has been deprecated
	Improved data types such as
	Edm.Time have been replaced with Edm.Duration and Edm.Time of Day
Date format was not existing	Edm.Date has been added
	Edm.Float has been eliminated
	Allows synchronous requests

The following request comparisons show the performance improvements from an OData V2 service compared to an OData V4 service request for the same type of request and using a free online OData service called Northwind and showcased in Figures 2-1 and 2-2.

One of the main differences in performance improvement between these two versions is the fact that the payload size in JSON format is relatively smaller in comparison to the same request returning an XML payload, as shown next.

Figure 2-1. *OData service v2*

```
  https://services.odata.org/V4/N×   +

  ←  →  C  ⌂      🔒 services.odata.org/V4/Northwind/Northwind.svc/Customers?$top=1

{
    @odata.context: "https://services.odata.org/V4/Northwind/Northwind.svc/$metadata#Customers",
  - value: [
      - {
              CustomerID: "ALFKI",
              CompanyName: "Alfreds Futterkiste",
              ContactName: "Maria Anders",
              ContactTitle: "Sales Representative",
              Address: "Obere Str. 57",
              City: "Berlin",
              Region: null,
              PostalCode: "12209",
              Country: "Germany",
              Phone: "030-0074321",
              Fax: "030-0076545"
        }
    ]
}
```

Figure 2-2. *OData service v4*

2) OData Entities

The entities exposed in an OData service are
pointers to exposed back-end data models that
can further be used for CRUD (Create, Read,
Update, Delete) operations. The back-end data
models represent CDS views, tables, or other entry
points that a client application can interact with
the back end via the HTTP(s) protocol. You can
identify the different endpoints as Entity Sets in an
OData Service. You can see these Entity Sets while
requesting the metadata for the OData service as
shown in Figure 2-3.

3)   OData metadata

When an OData service is created, its contract
is represented as metadata of the same service.
The OData service metadata can be located by
appending */$metadata* to the end of the OData
service URI. The metadata file is an XML generated
file, as shown in Figure 2-3.

Figure 2-3. *OData service metadata showing an Entity Set*

The metadata of the application is used when mapping an SAP Fiori
application to a control such as a list or a table, and it uses the metadata of
the service to type of control and some of the properties to be bound, such
as record count, title of the data to be represented, labels for the filters, and
also ability to interpret data type for the control(s) to be used in the filter
bar in the case of a smart table in a List Report or Worklist template. These
additional properties can be seen in Figure 2-4.

Figure 2-4. *OData metadata*

In addition to the ***Entity Set*** (endpoint) and the ***Entity Type*** (endpoint definition), the OData service also provides navigation properties. In the case of the Products Entity Set, we can observe that it has three navigation property bindings in Figure 2-5.

a) Navigation property binding to the Category target

b) Navigation property binding to the Order_Details target

c) Navigation property binding to the Supplier target

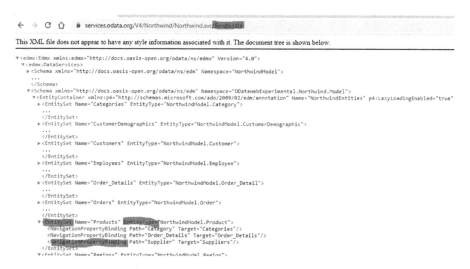

Figure 2-5. *OData service metadata showing Entity Set*

What does it mean to have a navigation binding? If you guessed that it allows these entities to have relationships defined between the endpoints, you guessed correctly. The navigation property is a simple way to understand and follow data relationships from one endpoint to another. This is a very common scenario on applications where a list of data is displayed, then the user of the application wishes to drill down or *navigate* to an item to find out more details about a specific record.

One of the other used URL syntax features is the need to know the record count of an entity. In order to retrieve the record count, please see Figure 2-6.

Figure 2-6. *OData service showing record count*

When testing out these OData services, developers can perform several types of requests to validate the web service they are consuming. These different ways to validate an OData service use different query syntax URLs provided by the OData protocol. The most common ones are shown in Table 2-2:

Table 2-2. *OData Operations and Operators*

Description of test	URL Syntax
Get Service definition	URL/Path
Get metadata	URL/Path/**$metadata**
Get top N results	URL/Path?**$top**=N → N is a positive integer
Get Entity	URL/Path/**Entity** → Get all records from **Entity.** Be careful when retrieving an entire Entity Set
Filter Entity by property	URL/Path/Entity?**$filter**={Prop} **eq** '{SomeValue}' • The $filter operator allows filtering by a property {Prop} • {SomeValue} represents a value than can be understood by the {Prop} being filtered by • **eq** (equal) is one of many operators that can be applied to a filter query; other operators that can be used are **ne** not equal **gt** greater than **lt** less than **contains**
Get count of records	URL/Path/**$count** → returns the number of records from an entity
Formatting data to JSON or XML	URL/Path?**$format=json** → XML is the default format in OData v2 or JSON is default in V4

More information about the OData protocol and the OData service specification is found on their website at https://www.odata.org/.

One benefit of being able to use OData while binding data to any of the SAPUI5 tables is that the UI5 framework understands how to build these requests and it makes them behind the scenes, taking the complexity away from the developer building the application. Further, the table control, as well as other controls that represent a list-like behavior, can be set for pagination, scroll to load, and other events triggering similar OData requests to retrieve data from the OData service when it is required. The reason behind making smaller requests is to avoid a huge data set being pulled and to increase performance while the user is navigating the data and loading data on demand. In Chapter 3, we will showcase how some of these controls build smaller OData requests, and we will show the Network tab from the browser to compare network requests and their response times.

So far, the book has explained the OData protocol and a very common free sample OData service most developers are familiar with; the only purpose of it was to demonstrate the protocol, and how the request and response operations from these services work.

How would we approach the same situation if we were starting to develop an application, however, in a case in which certain situations may prevent a developer from connecting directly to an OData service? These are real scenarios that happen every day and that developers may encounter when starting to develop new applications. If you can generate a metadata file, then you could simulate the data with the mock data feature of the SAP Web IDE.

Let us proceed to showcase this same scenario of mocking the data. If you have an OData service and you can query its metadata XML file, start from there. In the next example, I am going to use an SAP HANA XSA OData service, which is explained with more details in the following. For now, let us analyze the metadata file and see how we can mock this data.

1) Access the service and retrieve the metadata file as shown in Figure 2-7

2) Copy the metadata XML file to a notepad file. Make sure there are no special characters in the XML payload that was generated, such as arrows or encoded XML

3) In the SAP Web IDE, create a new file inside your project within the SAPUI5 module, inside the *localService* folder, call it *metadata.xml*, and copy the generated XML that you previously copied into a Notepad file

4) Save the metadata.xml file

Figure 2-7. *OData metadata file added as localService*

In this file, the reader can observe the generated metadata and the properties from an endpoint. Next, right-click the metadata XML file and select *Edit Mock Data* as shown in Figure 2-8.

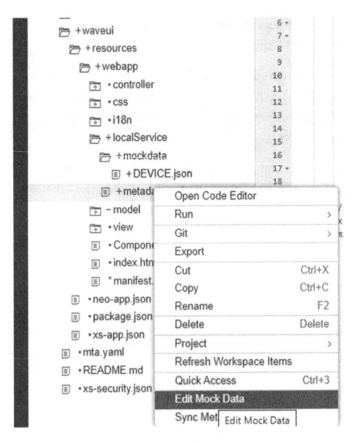

Figure 2-8. *Edit mock data*

Depending on your metadata file, it will generate one or more Entity Sets, as shown in Figure 2-9 for my metadata file with one endpoint.

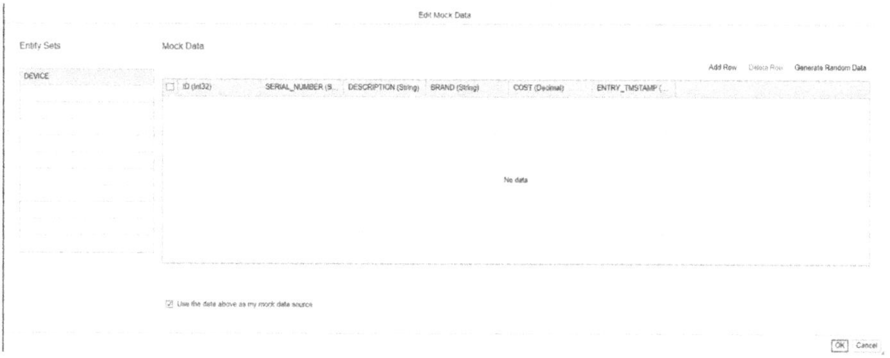

Figure 2-9. *Mock data wizard*

If you click the top right-hand button, **Generate Random Data**, the wizard will generate some mocked data according to your metadata file definition. From this wizard, developers may use the data as is, or they can edit the data in each cell if they wish. Additional data can be added by selecting the **Add Row** button or **Delete Row** if that is the desired output, as shown in Figure 2-10.

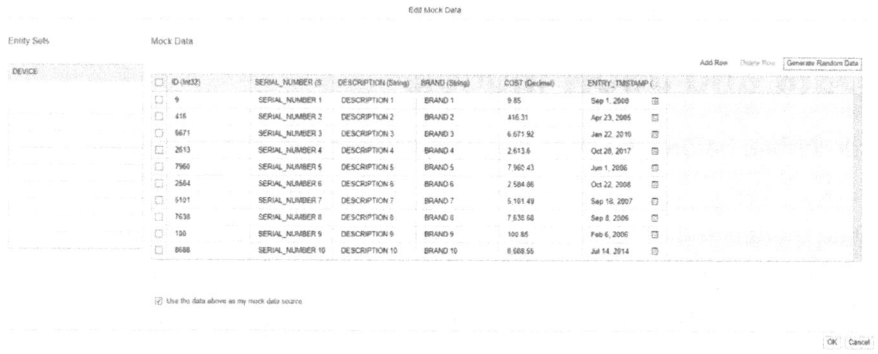

Figure 2-10. *Generate Random Data*

As soon as the developer clicks the **OK** button, the generated data is saved as a JSON file within the *localService* folder, as shown in Figure 2-11.

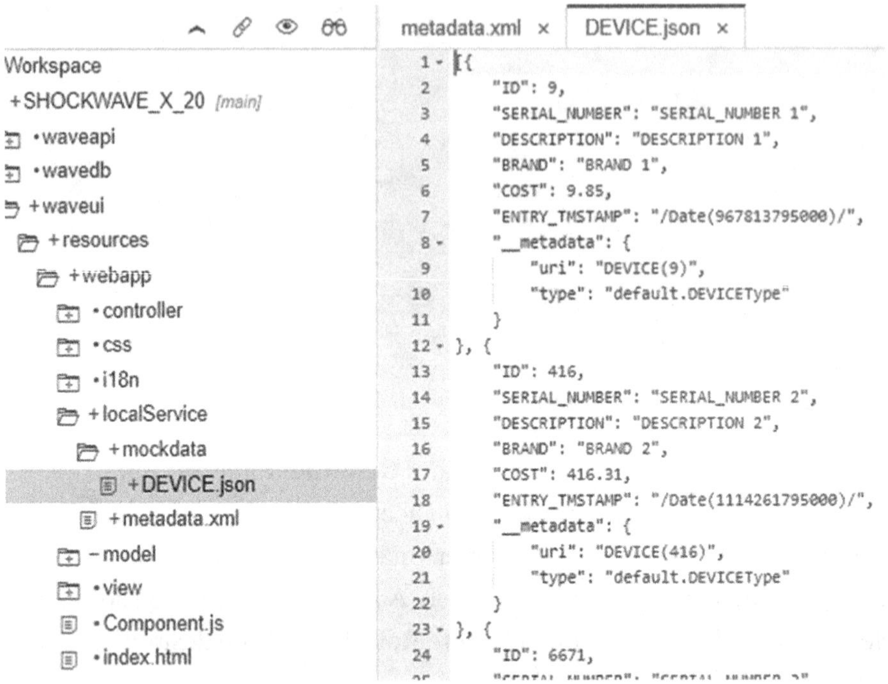

Figure 2-11. *Sample JSON data generated*

OData and JSON Models

As described before, the OData protocol allows fast retrieval of data from a back-end system that exposes endpoints as entities. All interaction from OData models is done from the client (browser or application) and the server that is exposing these endpoints. There may be use cases where a developer needs to simulate some data, update it, and reflect it on the screen without having to post it to the back-end server. In these types of situations, developers can use a different model called a JSON model. A JSON model is a client-side model that allows manipulation of data from an application and does not necessarily require it to be sent it back to a server. Scenarios such as those requiring client-side data simulations are perfect for this type of use case.

From the point of view of the SAPUI5 controls, it does not matter if the controls need to use an OData model or a JSON model. SAPUI5 applications support both JSON and OData models. The only differentiator when multiple models are present is that there needs to be named models when binding to a control or aggregation.

A named model is one that has a specific name (instead of the default empty string). Named models are specified in the SAPUI5 application manifest file and then referenced from the XML views in an SAP Fiori application.

Continue to create an OData service to demonstrate the setup of an OData service. This example is done in an SAP HANA express edition landscape running in XS Advance HANA 2 SPS04. The book assumes the developer already has access to this type of system whether it is in an on-premise environment or in some cloud instance. The setup for an SAP HANA XSA API can also be read from my other book titled *Microservices in SAP HANA XSA* (Apress, 2020).

Assume you have created an application in HANA XSA, and you have created an OData service called shockwaveSvc.xsodata. Following the preceding steps to see the metadata and the endpoints exposed first, let us look at this OData service metadata and definition in Figure 2-12.

Figure 2-12. *OData service definition*

Currently, there is a single endpoint called **DEVICE** and it was exposed in the **shockwaveSvc.xsodata** service, as shown in Figure 2-13.

Notice that an XSA OData service can be defined as a single XSOData service, or an SAP HANA XS OData service can also contain multiple entities. Within this service we have an entity called **wavex20.wavedb. data::tbls.DEVICE**. This entity represents a CDS HANA table, called *tbls. DEVICE*, inside the **wavedb** database module of my **wavex20** MTA (**M**ulti-**T**argeted **A**pplication) project.

By default, the XSOData service accepts all CRUD (Create, Read, Update, and Delete) operations; however, I have added a line of code to forbid the deletion of records from this endpoint. We will explore more about the forbidden command in the next chapter.

Figure 2-13. *XS OData service*

After creating the XSOData service, setting up a route in the xs-app. json file of the HTML5 module and activating the service, we can then navigate to it from the browser (or POSTMAN REST client).

Figure 2-14 shows the GET request from the Chrome browser.

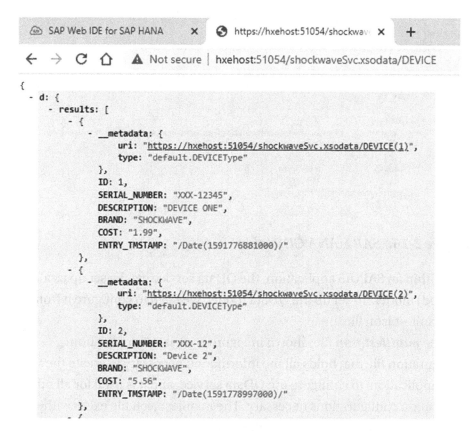

Figure 2-14. *OData GET request*

In the sample request, we can observe a few more things:

1) The **DEVICE** endpoint has the **ID** property as *key.*

2) The *key* property is used for navigation to a single entry as well.

3) The properties for each record are also shown in the metadata operation and the data types are shown correctly.

The table definition for the same endpoint is shown in Figure 2-15.

```
shockwaveSvc.xsodata  ×      tbls.hdbcds  ×
 1   namespace wavex20.wavedb.data;
 2
 3 ▾ context tbls {
 4
 5 ▸     ENTITY TBL {⬚};
10
11 ▾     ENTITY DEVICE {
12             KEY ID            : Integer generated always as identity (start with 1 increment by 1);
13             SERIAL_NUMBER     : String(32);
14             DESCRIPTION       : String(100);
15             BRAND             : String(100);
16             COST              : Decimal(5,2);
17             ENTRY_TMSTAMP     : UTCDateTime;
18         };
19
```

Figure 2-15. *SAP HANA CDS table*

Within an SAPUI5 application, the OData service can be set up as a (named) model. To set up the OData model, we need to configure it from the manifest.json file.

The ***manifest.json*** file, shown in Figure 2-16, is the application configuration file that holds all the information necessary to create the SAP Fiori application, to configure the OData service, and it is used for all other application configurations necessary. The manifest.json file exists within the HTML5 module of an MTA application.

Figure 2-16. *manifest.json file*

The manifest file is broken down into three sections:

a) The **sap.app** section contains information about the ui5 version, any dependencies, and data sources.

b) The **sap.ui** section contains information about the user interface and setup, including what types of devices can display it.

c) The **sap.ui5** section contains details about the SAPUI5 application and its views, among other properties.

To set up the named model, you must include the data source within the sap.app section and specify the URL where this OData service is located. There are a few scenarios that can be set up here:

1) In an SAP HANA XSA application where the OData service exists in a module within the same project, we can reference the OData service via a relative path.

2) In an SAP Fiori application running in the front-end server (NetWeaver front end and ABAP back end), we can also reference the relative path of the OData service as long as the application and the OData service live in the same domain/host. The same concept applies if the Fiori application is deployed to the SAP Cloud Platform in a neo-app.json file.

3) In the scenario where the OData we need exists outside of our domain/landscape, then we must include the fully qualified URL of that OData service as is the case for the Northwind OData service we used in the previous section as an example.

Once the OData service is included in the manifest file, then we can reference it as a named model using the correct name from the sap. ui5/**models** section, as shown in Figure 2-16. Notice also we have another named model called i18n; this model is used in most UI5 applications when internationalization is required.

In Chapter 3 we will go deeper into the named models and how they work in an SAPUI5 Fiori application; however, as a quick reference, the user interface binds to the named model as shown in the code snipper in Figure 2-17.

The example uses an SAPUI5 list control to show a list of **DEVICE** records, and the items in the list are bound to the **shockwave>** named model and the **DEVICE** endpoint. Each of the items is a Standard List Item control, and the title is bound to the **shockwave>** named model, using the **SERIAL_NUMBER** and **DESCRIPTION** properties of the model.

```
<List
    headerText="Devices"
    items="{
        path: 'shockwave>/DEVICE'
    }" >
    <StandardListItem
        title="{shockwave>SERIAL_NUMBER} {shockwave>DESCRIPTION}" />
</List>
```

Figure 2-17. *SAPUI5 list control*

When the named model is used in the SAPUI5 application, we can see the OData request from the browser by using the browser developer tools (F12) and clicking the network tab.

In Figure 2-18, you can see the initial fetch of data from the application by calling the XSOData service at the location below along with the request method, the status code, and also the remote address where the XSOData service lives. All these properties are important to know when developing or consuming an OData service and an SAP Fiori application.

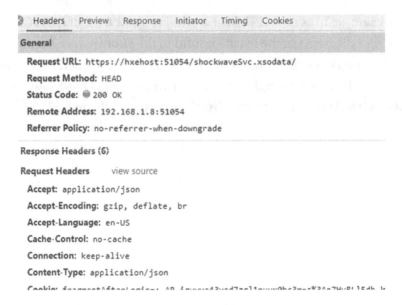

Figure 2-18. *Chrome browser network request*

Since this scenario uses a real OData service, then we can immediately see the data when we bind an SAPUI5 control to the named model. Figure 2-19 uses the same control from Figure 2-17.

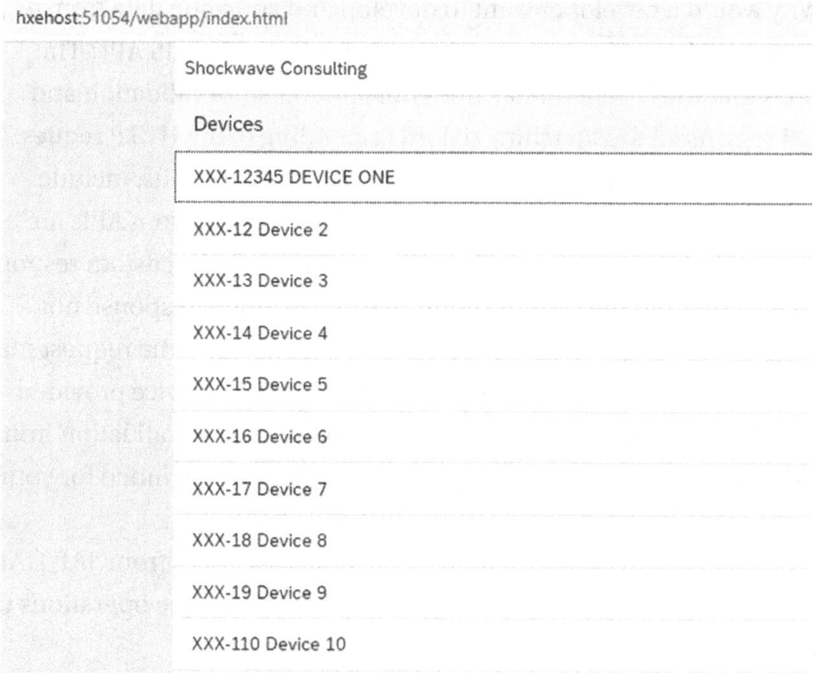

hxehost:51054/webapp/index.html

Shockwave Consulting

Devices

XXX-12345 DEVICE ONE

XXX-12 Device 2

XXX-13 Device 3

XXX-14 Device 4

XXX-15 Device 5

XXX-16 Device 6

XXX-17 Device 7

XXX-18 Device 8

XXX-19 Device 9

XXX-110 Device 10

Figure 2-19. *OData used in an SAPUI5 application*

Consuming REST APIs

REpresentational **S**tate **T**ransfer (REST) Application Programming Interfaces (APIs) are web services that are used for handling custom logic when requesting data from an API call, unlike OData services, which only take the HTTP(s) request and return data when a query matches data in the back end or returns zero records if no matching requests exist.

In the following example, the book uses a NodeJS microservice (REST API) to return data from the same entity, DEVICE. The difference between the OData endpoint returning the data directly from the table and the Node JS microservice API is that the Node JS API takes the incoming request, analyzes it, and then calls a data model built as a calculation view in SAP HANA, querying the same table and then returning the data as a JSON array.

Why would a developer want to develop and consume data from a custom endpoint such as the one described using a Node JS API? The reason is that the OData service does not allow custom validation and the API returns all the matching records according to the HTTP request. In certain scenarios when the API requires to validate inputs, include business logic, or have a custom response, then these custom APIs are a better approach to consider. Giving the caller of the API a custom response makes a bigger difference than simply getting an empty response not knowing if the filter parameters were correct or valid or if the request may have been missing required information. In an OData service provided by an ABAP stack, the OData service can provide custom validation from an ABAP class. This is out of the scope of the book, but included for your reference.

When consuming these custom APIs or microservices from SAP HANA or any other system, there are multiple ways in which these operations can be achieved:

1) Using the SAUI5 framework and considering a JSON model

2) Using a JQuery asynchronous JavaScript (AJAX) operation for asynchronous calls from the Fiori application toward a REST API

Since we have included a comparison between the SAPUI5 framework and the JQuery JavaScript framework, let us compare similarities and differences in Table 2-3.

Table 2-3. *SAPUI5 vs JQuery framework comparison*

SAPUI5	JQuery AJAX
It is a framework developed by SAP that provides HTML5/CSS3 controls and is used by SAP to create Fiori applications. Its controls have events that can be synchronous or asynchronous.	It is a small, fast JavaScript framework that allows manipulation of the DOM, event handling, and animation across browsers. It allows AJAX calls and it has a wide adoption by JavaScript developers.
It has an open source version called openui5.	It is an open source library.
It does not require JQuery but it can integrate with it.	It has different versions, for web, mobile, and unit testing.

There may be some issues that come up when consuming REST APIs. Some of the common scenarios include making requests outside of our network resulting in cross-domain request errors. To prevent cross-domain requests and to minimize the risk of attacks, certain measures can be included within a service/API. These measures include being able to guard against cross-domain requests, reject requests based on request headers, accept only requests from a specific domain, and accept requests that contain specific tokens, just to mention a few. From an SAP HANA XSA application we can set up the authentication type as route, certificate, or basic.

Route authentication means that the request made to/from an application needs to be validated by the UAA (user authentication and authorization) service as described in the Cloud Foundry specifications and as the same implementation is adopted by SAP HANA XSA. In my book *Microservices in SAP HANA XSA* (Apress, 2020), I explained in deep detail about the UAA service and how it is used within an SAP HANA XSA environment.

61

Additional situations for using models in a Fiori application can also include situations when there is no OData model (server side) and there needs to be a local (client-side) model. This type of model is known as a JSON model. JSON models allow for simulation of data, and the data in such a model does not need to be bound to the server. Developers can create JSON models in the following two ways:

1) Specifying the JSON model in the manifest.json file as shown in Figure 2-20.

```
manifest.json  ×
61              "sap.collaboration": {},
62              "sap.ui.comp": {},
63              "sap.uxap": {}
64            }
65          },
66 ▾       "contentDensities": {
67            "compact": true,
68            "cozy": true
69          },
70 ▾       "models": {
71 ›          "i18n": {⊙},
77 ›          "shockwave": {⊙},
85 ▾          "localModel" : {
86              "type" : "sap.ui.model.json.JSONModel"
87            }
88          },
```

Figure 2-20. *manifest.json file showing a local model*

Then using it from the application to read the model, set or get a specific property in the named model as shown in Figure 2-21.

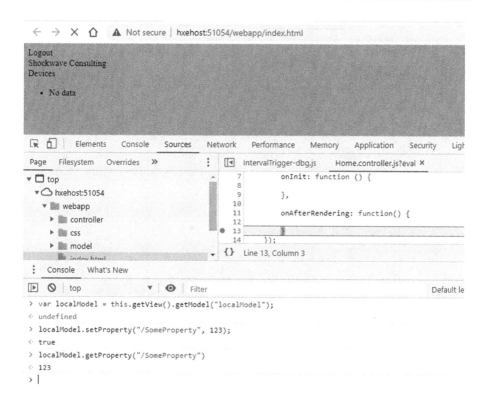

Figure 2-21. *Querying the named model from the browser console*

2) Creating a JSON model from the Component file like the i18n device model shown in Figure 2-22.

```
manifest.json  ×    Component.js  ×    models.js  ×
 1 ▾  sap.ui.define([
 2        "sap/ui/core/UIComponent",
 3        "sap/ui/Device",
 4        "shockwave/waveui/model/models"
 5 ▾  ], function (UIComponent, Device, models) {
 6        "use strict";
 7
 8 ▾      return UIComponent.extend("shockwave.waveui.Component", {
 9
10 ▾          metadata: {
11                  manifest: "json"
12              },
13
14 ▾          /**
15               * The component is initialized by UI5 automatically during the startup
16               * @public
17               * @override
18               */
19 ▾          init: function () {
20                  // call the base component's init function
21                  UIComponent.prototype.init.apply(this, arguments);
22
23                  // enable routing
24                  this.getRouter().initialize();
25
26                  // set the device model
27                  this.setModel(models.createDeviceModel(), "device");
28              }
29          });
30  });
```

Figure 2-22.   *i18n device model*

Using the models.js file as shown in Figure 2-23.

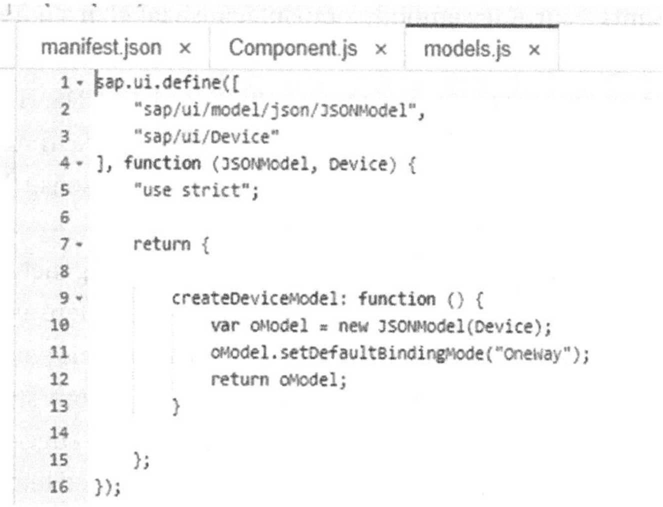

```
manifest.json  ×    Component.js  ×    models.js  ×

 1 ▾ sap.ui.define([
 2          "sap/ui/model/json/JSONModel",
 3          "sap/ui/Device"
 4 ▾ ], function (JSONModel, Device) {
 5          "use strict";
 6
 7 ▾      return {
 8
 9 ▾          createDeviceModel: function () {
10              var oModel = new JSONModel(Device);
11              oModel.setDefaultBindingMode("OneWay");
12              return oModel;
13          }
14
15      };
16 });
```

Figure 2-23.   models.js file setting the device model

OData-Driven Design Approaches

Thus far we have discussed the OData services when there is data available and mocking data when we do not have data directly accessible, but we can also generate data from an OData metadata file. We also consumed data from a REST API microservice. Wouldn't it also make sense to have our SAP Fiori application to provide a data-driven solution to be able to create these Enterprise applications with little to no effort?

Smart Controls are control templates within the SAPUI5 SDK (Software Development Kit) that provide this type of feature and behavior. These templates use metadata XML files and annotations that understand the metadata and can transform these XML annotations and metadata into actual SAPUI5 applications and Fiori elements.

Annotations are additional properties that use a semantic meaning to properties within an OData endpoint. The sole purpose of giving additional meaning to some data is to enrich the meaning of the data itself; for example, adding currency symbols to a decimal number that truly represents a currency amount, or displaying a label in a different format such as all caps. Annotations in SAP HANA CDS contain limited set types of annotations compared to those in SAP ABAP CDS. HANA CDS and ABAP CDS are very similar in the sense that they derive from the same scripting language; however, they are very different in the sense that not all annotation types apply in both technologies.

When should these types of applications be built (using metadata and annotations instead of actual XML and JavaScript)? There are design guidelines to consider if the desired behavior is to follow this path. If the development of applications is very standard, design consistency is needed, and not much customization is required, then the suggested way to create these applications is to follow these predefined templates. When you start your design phase and you notice some customization of your application, then the application being built may not be a good candidate for smart template development. Keep in mind that this type of development has a mandatory requirement of using OData services and the application to be built follows one of the Fiori elements discussed in Chapter 1 (List Report, Worklist, Overview page).

Let us proceed to build an Overview page using our existing OData service. As mentioned in Chapter 1, an Overview page is a quick look of the system with the purpose of giving the user a glance at what is going on in the data, in this case devices, without having to drill down into each specific app or tile to find out more.

In our data set represented by DEVICES, we also have a table that contains device metrics. The metrics captured here are temperature and date recorded. This data is simply for the exercise. I will start by building additional data models to represent the data we want to represent in the Overview page. In the Overview page, let's display the average temperature of the devices; in another section, we will display the cost of the devices in descending order. By looking at an example of the Overview page, we need to build sections called ***cards***.

Cards represent a small section of data within an Overview page and they contain a header where we can set the title, and then a content area to represent a table, a chart or graph, or some other text. There are a few different types of cards: analytical (has title and a measure), list, bar chart, table, and quick view (information content like a form).

Let's start by designing the data models in the database and adding them to the OData Service in order for the application to use them as cards in the Overview page. Figure 2-24 shows the data architecture at a high level using the DEVICE and DEVICE_METRICS tables, the CV_DEVICES and CV_AVG_TEMP_DEVICES calculation views, and finally the additional endpoint in the OData service.

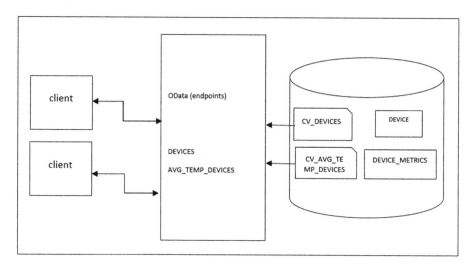

Figure 2-24. *Data architecture for AvgTmpDevices*

In the OData service, it looks like Figure 2-25.

```
ıL Console 1.sql  ×      shockwaveSvc.xsodata  ×

    service {
        "wavex20.wavedb.data::tbls.DEVICE" as "DEVICE"
        delete forbidden;


        "wavex20.wavedb.models::CV_AVG_TEMP_DEVICES" as "AVG_TEMP_DEVICES"
        create forbidden
        update forbidden
        delete forbidden;
    }
```

Figure 2-25. *XSOData service including additional endpoints*

And once they are exposed, the metadata file looks like Figure 2-26.

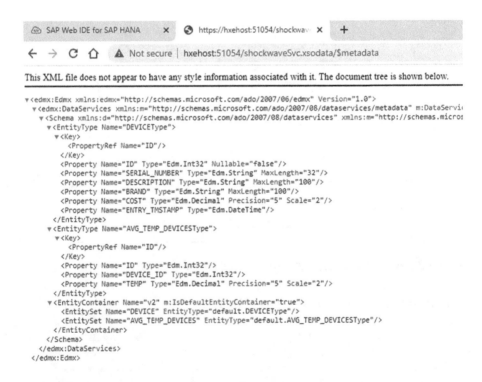

Figure 2-26. *OData service metadata*

Retrieving the data shows as Figure 2-27. From the data generated in the following, we need to leverage the SAPUI5 controls, binding to the data and sorting the data in descending order using the TEMP property.

```
≥  SAP Web IDE for SAP HANA     ×  |  ⬤ https://hxehost:51054/shockwav  ×      ⬤ https://hxehost:51054/shockwav  ×

→  C  ⌂   ▲ Not secure |  hxehost:51054/shockwaveSvc.xsodata/AVG_TEMP_DEVICES?$format=json

d: {
  - results: [
    - {
      - __metadata: {
          uri: "https://hxehost:51054/shockwaveSvc.xsodata/AVG_TEMP_DEVICES(1)",
          type: "default.AVG_TEMP_DEVICESType"
        },
        ID: 1,
        DEVICE_ID: 1,
        TEMP: "52.666666666666666666666666666667"
      },
    - {
      - __metadata: {
          uri: "https://hxehost:51054/shockwaveSvc.xsodata/AVG_TEMP_DEVICES(99)",
          type: "default.AVG_TEMP_DEVICESType"
        },
        ID: 99,
        DEVICE_ID: 99,
        TEMP: "104.3333333333333333333333333333333"
      },
    - {
      - __metadata: {
          uri: "https://hxehost:51054/shockwaveSvc.xsodata/AVG_TEMP_DEVICES(100)",
          type: "default.AVG_TEMP_DEVICESType"
        },
        ID: 100,
        DEVICE_ID: 100,
        TEMP: "92"
      }
    ]
}
```

Figure 2-27. *OData AvgTmpDevices endpoint*

From here, then the metadata file and the annotations need to be generated (if doing local development; otherwise, developers can proceed and connect to an existing OData service).

Using the SAP Web IDE (either personal edition or full stack version from SAP Cloud or the SAP Business Application Studio), we can use the Create new application wizard as shown in Figure 2-28.

Figure 2-28. *Template Selection wizard*

From this screen, select the Overview page and follow the wizard to create the Overview page as shown in Figure 2-29.

Figure 2-29. *New Overview page step*

Once the properties are added, then select the OData service or a metadata file as shown in Figure 2-30.

Figure 2-30. *Data connection step*

After selecting the endpoints, then the user can create an annotation file as shown in Figure 2-31, or this step can be skipped now and created later.

Figure 2-31. *Annotation selection step*

Continue by selecting the ***Datasource Alias*** and the ***EntityType*** as shown in Figure 2-32. These properties are saved to the manifest.json file.

Figure 2-32. *Template customization step*

After finishing those steps, the developer can see the additional changes reflected in the workspace project, as shown in Figure 2-33.

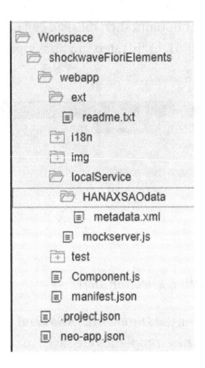

Figure 2-33. *Project structure*

Since we are going to be using the XML metadata file, then, proceed to edit the mock data, and we should be able to follow the steps shown in Figure 2-34.

Workspace
shockwaveFioriElements
webapp
ext
readme.txt
i18n
img
localService
HANAXSAOdata
metadata.xml
test
manifest.json
.project.json
neo-app.json
New
Open With
Edit Mock Data
Import
Export
Cut
Ctrl+X
Edit Mock Data

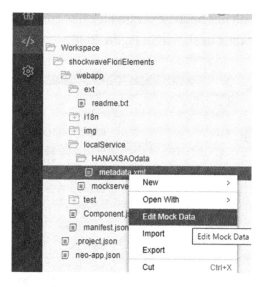

Figure 2-34. *Edit mock data*

The generated mock data is displayed in Figure 2-35.

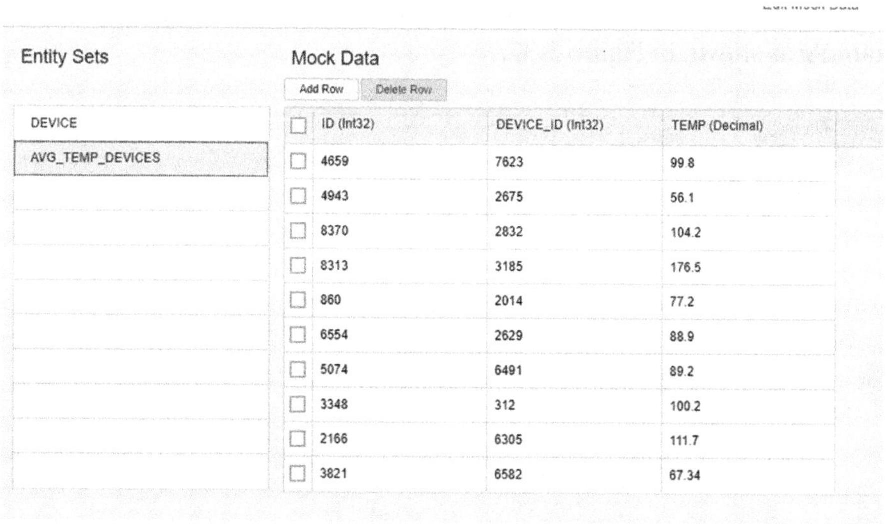

Entity Sets
Mock Data
Add Row
Delete Row
DEVICE
AVG_TEMP_DEVICES
ID (Int32)
DEVICE_ID (Int32)
TEMP (Decimal)
4659 7623 99.8
4943 2675 56.1
8370 2832 104.2
8313 3185 176.5
860 2014 77.2
6554 2629 88.9
5074 6491 89.2
3348 312 100.2
2166 6305 111.7
3821 6582 67.34

Figure 2-35. *Sample mock data*

Now that the data has been generated locally, continue to create a **card** to display this data as shown in Figure 2-36.

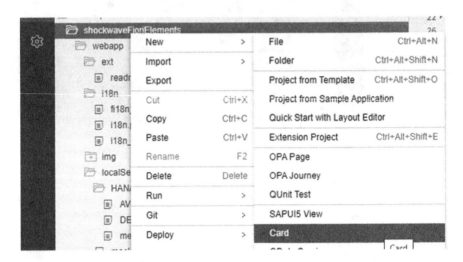

Figure 2-36. *Adding a new card control*

Different types of cards are presented; select the List card for this example as shown in Figure 2-37.

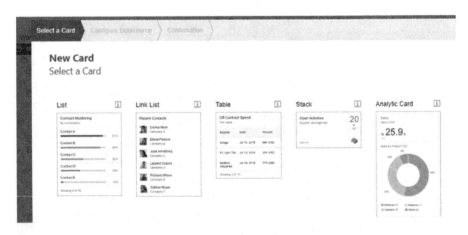

Figure 2-37. *Selecting card type*

After selecting the card, proceed to selecting a data source and an endpoint to the data to be displayed in the card, as shown in Figure 2-38.

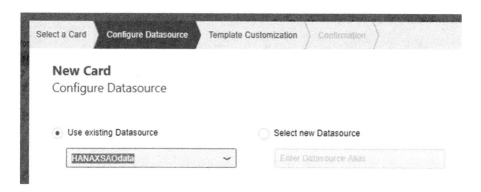

Figure 2-38. *Card configuration for data source*

Confirm the card properties to set up the *Avg Temp* for the devices as shown in Figures 2-39 and 2-40, respectively.

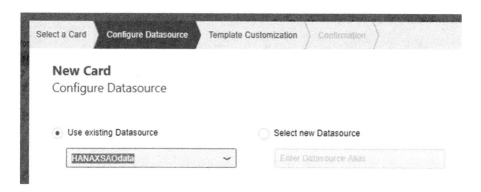

Figure 2-39. *Card template configuration*

The most important part of the card setup, in my opinion, is related to the next screenshot where we display list item information and display and sort configuration as well.

Figure 2-40. *Card configuration continues*

The same configuration is stored in the manifest.json file as displayed in Figure 2-41.

```
readme.txt ×      testOVP.html ×      manifest.json ×
58 ▾              "HANAXSAOdata": {
59                    "dataSource": "HANAXSAOdata",
60 ▾                  "settings": {
61                        "defaultCountMode": "Inline"
62                    }
63                }
64            },
65 ▾         "extends": {
66              "extensions": {}
67            },
68 ▾         "contentDensities": {
69              "compact": true,
70              "cozy": true
71            }
72        },
73 ▾      "sap.ovp": {
74            "globalFilterModel": "HANAXSAOdata",
75            "globalFilterEntityType": "AVG_TEMP_DEVICESType",
76            "containerLayout": "fixed",
77            "enableLiveFilter": true,
78            "considerAnalyticalParameters": false,
79 ▾         "cards": {
80 ▾             "card00": {
81                    "model": "HANAXSAOdata",
82                    "template": "sap.ovp.cards.list",
83 ▾                  "settings": {
84                        "title": "{{card00_title}}",
85                        "subTitle": "{{card00_subTitle}}",
86                        "entitySet": "AVG_TEMP_DEVICES",
87                        "listType": "condensed",
88                        "listFlavor": "standard",
89                        "sortBy": "TEMP",
90                        "sortOrder": "descending",
91                        "addODataSelect": false,
92 ▾                      "tabs": [
93 ▾                          {
94                                "value": "1"
95                            },
96 ▾                          {
97                                "value": "2"
98                            }
```

Figure 2-41. *Manifest file showing the card configuration*

Since annotations were not added during the initial project setup, now is the time to do so. Select the project, right-click it, and select the add annotations option. Figure 2-42 shows the annotation configuration wizard. This step is usually done if you did not have an annotations file previously.

Figure 2-42. *Annotation file configuration*

Select the type of annotation as presented in Figure 2-43.

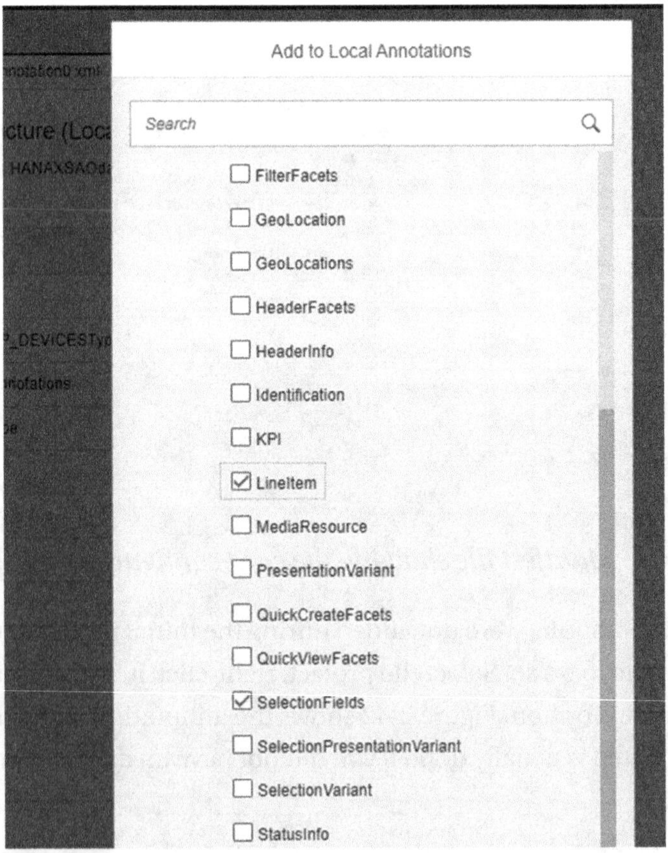

Figure 2-43. *Annotation types*

And confirm the annotation completion.

Open the annotation XML file and notice the placeholders for **Selection fields** and **LineItem** inside the XML file. The UI.SelectionField represents fields to be used for the filtering of data, while the UI.LineItem annotation represents an object collection that will be filtered. You will need to add the following sections to be able to search and to display the data in the card control of the Overview page as shown in Figure 2-44.

Figure 2-44. *Annotation XML file*

Once these properties are added, select the project, and run as Overview test page to see how it would display in the Fiori Launchpad as it was in our setup for the current exercise. The data at the moment makes no sense, as it was a generated JSON file from the Web IDE; however, you can add relevant text in the JSON file or when directly connected to the back-end service providing that the data will actually display relevant information (Figure 2-45).

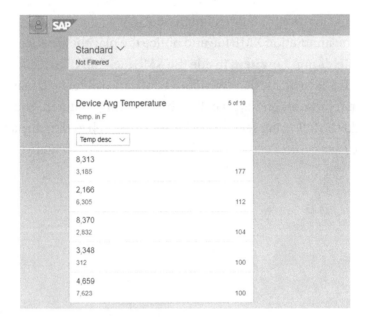

Figure 2-45. *Card shown in Overview page*

Conclusion

As the book concludes this chapter, I would like to highlight the importance of using data in an application and the various ways to consume data, such as OData services and REST APIs. When there is no data present, developers can still generate local JSON models or use the metadata file to mock some data from the SAP Web IDE. The local mock data feature has huge benefits and it is sometimes common to start development activities when actual data is not present for the application developer. Moreover, additional points within the chapter that are of huge importance are the different pieces of making data integration to an SAP Fiori application. Understanding the different types of application templates, Fiori elements, and layouts will be helpful in the next chapter, when we dive deeper into more custom Fiori development. Keep also in mind how data is represented as data models and how those data models are bound to applications.

CHAPTER 3

Building the Fiori Application

Welcome to Chapter 3, the developer chapter. Thank you for following along the first two chapters, where the book explained the required steps to start a custom SAP Fiori application starting from the design phase and then analyzing and playing with data or even simulating it when data is not available. This chapter focuses on the actual implementation of an SAP Fiori application and primarily focuses on the developer. In this chapter, the book dives deeper into the different areas that make up a Fiori application; it explains the software design pattern known as MVC (Model View Controller) and the different tools for developing and debugging such as the SAP Web IDE. It also talks about integrating third-party JavaScript libraries into our SAP Fiori web application, and then it shows various scenarios as to how the Fiori application is seen from different devices such as desktops, tablets, and phone devices.

MVC

The MVC architectural design pattern has been around for a very long time. Its popularity in software has been incredible since its introduction in the 70s–80s. It was originally developed with the intent of decoupling software, to allow separation of concerns from the code point of view,

© Sergio Guerrero 2021
S. Guerrero, *Custom Fiori Applications in SAP HANA*,
https://doi.org/10.1007/978-1-4842-6358-7_3

and it has evolved into different flavors of the initial pattern, such as MVP (Model View Presenter) and MVVM (Model View View Model). This architectural pattern has been adopted by various programming languages such as C#, JavaScript, PHP, NodeJS, and Java, just to mention a few.

This book will focus on MVC and how it applies to SAP Fiori applications using the SAPUI5 library. In Table 3-1, we can observe some advantages and disadvantages of the design pattern.

Table 3-1. *Advantages and Disadvantages of Using MVC*

Advantages	Disadvantages
Loose coupling of code files	It can be overwhelming depending on the complexity/size of the project
Multiple developers working simultaneously	Keeping track of who is doing what and code merging can be hectic
Multiple versions of a model	Learning curve can be challenging for new teams
Easier unit testing	Some less experienced developers struggle with the idea of decoupling code and modularization
Code reuse due to modularization	

The MVC pattern is usually depicted as a connected line between three sections, as shown in Figure 3-1.

1. The **Model** represents the data that comes from an API, a web service, or a local JSON model. In the case of Fiori applications, most of the time, the application references an OData service (server-side models), as shown in Chapter 2. These models can also be local to the application as JSON models (client-side models). The data models can be bound to the views

part of the pattern and reflect how the models are updated directly when the view uses a two-way binding. Binding can be done as a one-way binding, which means the application does a read-only of the model, or a two-way binding, which means the model can get updated from the view and the model always reflects the changes done by the views.

2. The **View** represents the HTML5 controls that are visualized by a user when working on an SAP Fiori application. The views bind to the model and immediately reflect the data model to the user. The user interface allows the user to interact with the model, and through events, the views call (notify) the controller to execute some behavior (such as calling a JavaScript function).

    Views can be created as HTML, XML, JSON, and JavaScript views. XML views is the preferred and suggested method by SAP. The reason to use XML views is that the application structure is more readable, and the XML views are also easily shown in the layout editor. Years ago, when SAPUI5 was introduced, JavaScript views were the original way of creating applications; however, due to complexity and language syntax, then they immediately became option number two.

3. The **Controller** gets triggered as a response to one or more events bound to the views. The view (HTML/XML/JavaScript) controls have different types of events depending on the control type. When the views trigger the events, JavaScript functions get executed in the corresponding controller.js file.

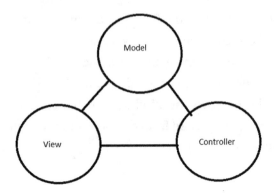

Figure 3-1. *MVC architecture pattern*

As mentioned in the previous paragraph, depending on the type of control used, they may have different types of events. Some of the common controls and events are presented in Table 3-2.

Table 3-2. *Common SAPUI5 controls*

Control Type	Event	Comment
Button	Press	When the user clicks the button
Input	onKeyUp, onKeyDown	When the user types
ComboBox	onSelectionChanged	When the user changes the item selection
Table	onItemPressed	When an item (row) is selected
List	onItemPressed	When a list item is pressed; this event is very similar in nature to the event in the responsive table control

These events can be used directly from the framework or from additional custom binding from within the application. Binding custom events to controls is a common activity if the desired event is not offered by the framework. It could be the case if we wanted to bind a scroll event to the application or invoke multiple events from the same control. Some use cases could be adding a keyUp, keyDown, mouse-over (hovering over the input element), or blur (when it loses focus) event on an SAPUI5 input field.

When working with the SAPUI5 library, developers can see the control-specific events if they navigate to the (UI5) *API Reference* tab. Look for a specific control from the Master list (shown on the left side navigation) and then you can see the control *Events* (shown in the detail section of the application at the right-hand side), as shown in Figure 3-2.

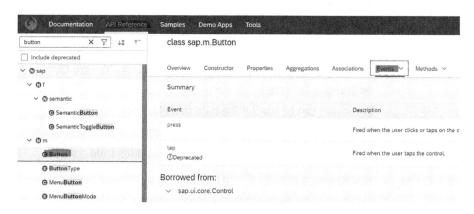

Figure 3-2. *SAPUI5 SDK API Reference tab*

Dedicate some time and navigate through a few of the other controls to familiarize yourself with the different types of events, and the difference in events from one control to another. You do not need to memorize each one of these events or properties of each control; however, it is helpful to understand where to find more information related to it within the SDK. Moreover, each UI5 element can also be attached to a browser element. The framework is very flexible in such a way that custom events can be included to these controls, such as scrolling of the page, mouse events, and before/after rendering.

Apart from single controls having these events, there are also events that occur during the life cycle of the application as is the case for views. Each view has a life cycle. Displayed in Table 3-3 are the view lifecycle events.

Table 3-3. *SAPUI5 view lifecycle events*

View event	When to use it
onInit	When the view gets initialized after navigating to it. This event is commonly used to initialize certain values to be used by the application. On certain occasions, the data model or the controls are not initialized yet until the next set of events. Beware and debug when using this event.
beforeRendering	The view has been initialized but not all the controls have been rendered to the screen. This event can be used if the data model is not ready yet during the onInit event and right before the controls are displayed on the screen. Other use cases can be to unbind events from controls.
afterRendering	The view was initialized, and the controls have been rendered to the screen and right before releasing control to the user. This event is helpful when the application needs to modify a control's behavior after those controls have been rendered to the screen. Further, this event can be used if we need to query the OData service and apply additional logic to the app.
beforeExit	Right before navigating away from or closing the view.

The same events can be found in the SAPUI5 SDK by looking up the XML view within the *API Reference* tab as shown in the following. Keep in mind that there may be events borrowed from other controls, as shown in Figure 3-3.

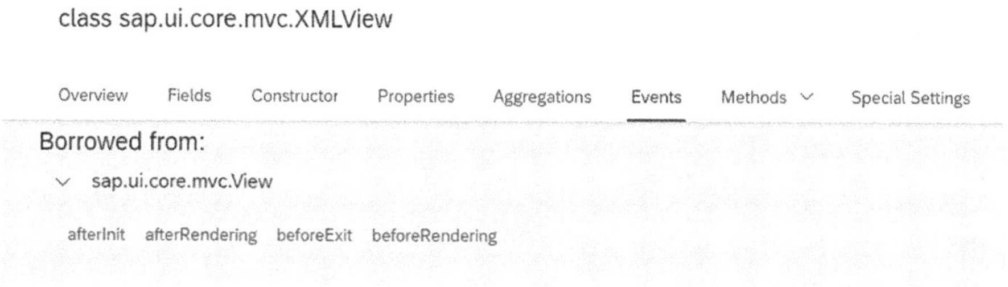

class sap.ui.core.mvc.XMLView

Overview	Fields	Constructor	Properties	Aggregations	Events	Methods ∨	Special Settings

Borrowed from:

∨   sap.ui.core.mvc.View

afterInit   afterRendering   beforeExit   beforeRendering

Figure 3-3. *XML view borrowed events*

Take a moment to open the SAP Web IDE and analyze some of the XML views to understand the MVC pattern and see how it applies when using SAPUI5. We will start by analyzing an application built in SAP HANA XSA express edition – HANA 2 XSA SPS04. This application showcases a master detail template approach. There are several views used within this Fiori application. The view contains several UI5 controls.

The master list contains a list of ***Devices*** from our XSOData service presented in Chapter 2. The **Master** view has a ***List*** control, and each of the list items is bound to the *items* aggregation. There are several events that can occur in this view. This master list can be seen in Figure 3-4.

1) Before binding the items (such is the case if the items need to be formatted before displaying them to the user interface)

2) Pressing on an item (for navigation or to display its details in the **Detail** view)

3) Searching on the list (to narrow down the displayed list)

Figure 3-4. *Master detail app*

The code to generate the preceding master detail template UI is shown in Figure 3-5.

```
Home.view.xml ×
1 +  <mvc:View xmlns:mvc="sap.ui.core.mvc" xmlns:html="http://www.w3.org/1999/xhtml" xmlns="sap.m" controllerName="shockwave.waveui.controller.Home" displayBlock="true">
2 +    <App id="idAppControl">
3 +      <pages>
4 +        <Page title="Shockwave Consulting">
5 +          <content>
6 +            <SplitApp>
7 +              <masterPages>
8 +                <Page showHeader="false" showFooter="false">
9 +                  <content>
10 +                   <List headerText="Devices" items="{ path: 'shockwave>/DEVICE' }">
11 +                     <items>
12                         <StandardListItem title="(shockwave>SERIAL_NUMBER} {shockwave&gt;DESCRIPTION}"/>
13                       </items>
14 +                     <headerToolbar>
15 +                       <Toolbar>
16 +                         <content>
17                             <Title text="Devices" title="Search"/>
18                             <ToolbarSpacer/>
19                             <SearchField search="onsearch" width="50%"/>
20 +                         </content>
21                         </Toolbar>
22                       </headerToolbar>
23                     </List>
24 +                 </content>
25                 </Page>
26               </masterPages>
27 +             <detailPages>
28 +               <Page showHeader="false">
29 +                 <content>
30 +                   <IconTabBar selectedKey="__filter0" id="bar0">
31 +                     <items>
32                         <IconTabFilter text="Active" count="10" icon="sap-icon://status-positive" iconColor="Positive" id="filter1"/>
33                         <IconTabFilter text="Inactive" count="5" icon="sap-icon://status-inactive" iconColor="Critical" id="filter2"/></items>
34                     </IconTabBar>
35                   </content>
36                 </Page>
37               </detailPages>
38             </SplitApp>
```

Figure 3-5. *XML view showing master detail template*

Notice that as more features are included into the application, the preceding **Home** view can get to be too busy and complex for any developer to understand. In Figure 3-6, the exercise shows the same application after refactoring the **Master** view page into its own view to show a cleaner setup of the view – refactoring is a normal practice during development when views or controllers start to get polluted or too busy during the application development. More experienced developers can easily help with refactoring and with the initial software design of the different files/modules of the application.

Figure 3-6. *MasterList XML view reference*

And the **MasterList** view definition is now located in the **View** folder, as shown in Figure 3-7. To generate the new view, right-click the **View** folder, select New, File, and provide the file name as well as the file content (you will need to copy the view declaration from the **Home** view into the newly created view). An alternative would be to use the provided "New SAPUI5 view" option from the SAP Web IDE to create the view and controller files into their respective folders.

Figure 3-7. *Project showing the **View** folder*

The **MasterList** view definition looks exactly as it did in the **Home** view before. The controller reference to the Home controller was kept as it was since this was a rather small example, and if required, the developer can add a new controller file inside the **Controller** folder and further update the view reference to the desired controller file location. This feature (new view and new controller) is shown in the **Detail** view example further in the following.

The **Detail** view may contain any control, form, item tab bar, or charts to display the selected item's detailed data. In this view, developers can observe that the tabs (item tab bar control) use the items aggregation and that there are events that can be triggered such as selecting an item. Situations such as including a filter can be helpful when these controls are used. The **Detail** view is shown in Figure 3-8 (after being refactored).

Figure 3-8. Detail view

And this (nested) **Detail** view is also referenced in the **Home** view, as
shown in Figure 3-9.

Figure 3-9. Detail view reference after refactoring

This is a great exercise to show case refactoring as well as to show developers that during development cycles, one can continue to refactor as one continues adding content to Fiori applications. You probably noticed that the **Detail** view is referencing the Detail controller and not the Home controller, as shown in line 2 of Figure 3-8. Moreover, the Detail controller lives inside the **Controller** folder, as shown in Figure 3-10.

Figure 3-10. *Detail controller*

Furthermore, an additional benefit of MVC is that its components are loosely coupled, and they can be reused in several parts of the application. Imagine that we have additional tabs, and within these tabs, the application requires to display the same control across tabs. You may wonder if the application could decouple the (UI5) control from the **Detail** view into a separate view and then embed the view that contains such a control inside the **Detail** view. Yes, it can.

Before refactoring the control that we want to split into its own view, the book will describe one feature of the SAPUI5 library, known as **Fragment**. As you have seen in the previous paragraphs, the book showed the views and each view may contain a controller with the same name. See Figure 3-10 to observe the view/controller in their corresponding folders. When developing these applications, developers should know that most times, each view file contains a corresponding controller file. Fragments behave like views; however, they do not contain a controller file. Instead, they are embedded within views and any events referenced within these fragments can be executed from the view's controller.

In Figure 3-11, you can observe that we have a responsive table control. This table control will display the activity for the devices under the Activity tab upon selection of a device from the master list. Furthermore, this table will also be used in the next tab to show inactivity of the devices. Instead of introducing repeated code, the exercise will refactor this snippet of XML code for the responsive table and it will refactor it into an XML fragment.

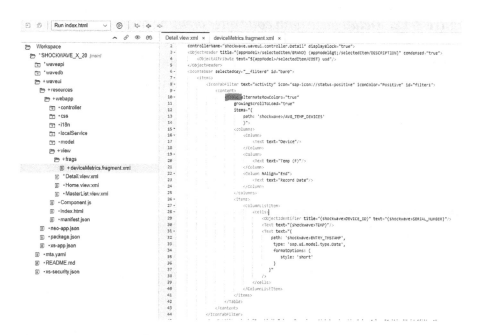

Figure 3-11. Detail *view with code before fragment*

In Figure 3-12, you can observe the refactored and clean piece of code within the **Detail** view again. When using a fragment, developers must ensure that the fragments contain unique ideas and they should provide a fragment name for easy access later from the JavaScript controller.

Figure 3-12. *Detail view with code after creating fragment*

If you are curious to see the fragment code definition, then look at Figure 3-13 to observe how easy it was to cut and move the code from the view into the fragment for reusability.

```
Detail.view.xml  ×    deviceMetrics.fragment.xml  ×
 1 • kcore:FragmentDefinition
 2        xmlns="sap.m"
 3        xmlns:core="sap.ui.core">
 4
 5 •      <Table alternateRowColors="true"
 6            growingScrollToLoad="true"
 7            items="{
 8                path: 'shockwave>/AVG_TEMP_DEVICES'
 9                }">
10 •        <columns>
11 •          <Column>
12               <Text text="Device"/>
13            </Column>
14 •          <Column>
15               <Text text="Temp (F)"/>
16            </Column>
17 •          <Column hAlign="End">
18               <Text text="Record Date"/>
19            </Column>
20          </columns>
21 •        <items>
22 •          <ColumnListItem>
23 •            <cells>
24                 <ObjectIdentifier title="{shockwave>DEVICE_ID}" text="{shockwave>SERIAL_NUMBER}"/>
25                 <Text text="{shockwave>TEMP}"/>
26 •              <Text text="{
27                     path: 'shockwave>ENTRY_TMSTAMP',
28                     type: 'sap.ui.model.type.Date',
29                     formatOptions: {
30                         style: 'short'
31                     }
32                 }"
33               />
34            </cells>
35          </ColumnListItem>
36        </items>
37      </Table>
38
39  </core:FragmentDefinition>
```

Figure 3-13. *Fragment definition*

Fragments are so versatile in the sense that they are snippets of code that can be reused within views and are more granular than views. Fragments are very common in standard SAP Fiori applications. Fragments as well as views and controllers are referenced by their namespace and file name. Neat, isn't it?

From the application, now we can see the same UI controls on both Activity and Inactivity tabs, as shown in Figures 3-14 and 3-15.

Note   Now the tabs display the same data; however, there will be some filter criteria applied so that the tab data makes more sense when using this application. The Activity tab will contain the TEMP metrics for devices where the TEMP value is greater than zero, while the Inactivity tab will contain metrics when the TEMP equals to zero.

Figure 3-14.   *Activity tab showing the fragment*

Figure 3-15.   *Inactivity tab shown the fragment*

Tools for Developing and Debugging Fiori Applications

In Chapters 2 and 3, we have been showcasing several tools that are used for development, and we have also shown debugging steps while developing an SAP Fiori application. Next, we would like to introduce some additional tools that developers may encounter, maybe on their next project.

The first, and most common, tool is the SAP Web IDE. There are several versions of this tool. Depending on the type of application you are going to build, there may be different license types that need to be considered. Look at the SAP Web IDE licensing details to decide which version is right for you or your organization.

The SAP Web IDE personal edition is one of the versions of the SAP Web IDE, and it is used for local development. It can be downloaded from the SAP tools page at `https://tools.hana.ondemand.com/#sapui5`. The login page looks like Figure 3-16.

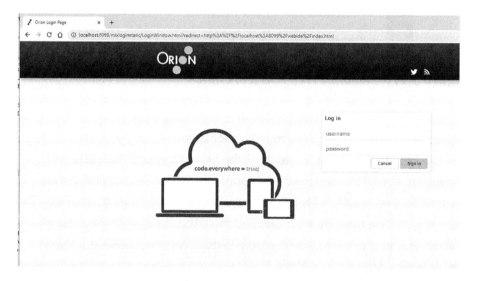

Figure 3-16. *SAP Web IDE personal edition*

After logging in to the **SAP Web IDE personal edition**, a developer is presented with the welcome page. From there, the developer can navigate to the workspace area where he/she will be working for the most part. Within the workspace, developers can create projects based on templates or create freestyle custom applications, as shown in Chapter 2 and in Figure 3-17.

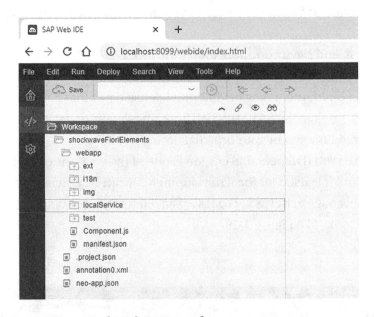

Figure 3-17. *Personal Web IDE workspace*

One or more projects can be created inside the workspace. All of these projects contain very similar project structures.

The next tool I would like to describe here is the **SAP Web IDE full stack** from the SAP cloud (and trial) platform (Figure 3-18). This version is a free version, and it is for the purpose of coming up with a sample SAP Fiori application to share with the readers of this book. Full stack means that developers can use it to develop UI5 applications, HANA database development objects, and Node JS APIs. There are many features offered from this tool, and I highly recommend that other developers invest time in understanding them (GIT integration, connecting to a HANA database, connecting to back-end ABAP systems, and debugging, just to mention a few of the many features offered).

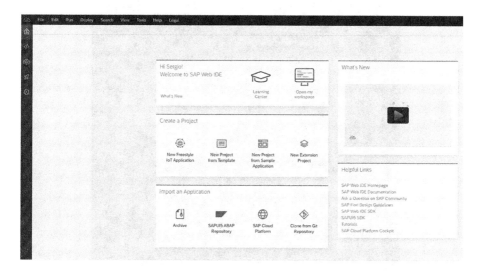

Figure 3-18. *SAP Web IDE full stack*

An additional advantage of using the SAP Web IDE tool is that it has a uniform look and feel across the different versions that it offers (cloud, on-premise, or personal edition). This is a huge plus, allowing developers to switch tools and still be able to continue their development as they progress from project to project or from client to client.

Another popular tool is Microsoft Visual Studio Code. This is a free code editor and IDE that can be used along with Fiori plug-ins that can be optionally installed. Visual Studio Code is probably the most robust IDE to date and it also can also be used for development in other languages (node, JavaScript, Go, Python). It is displayed in Figure 3-19. To install these plug-ins, open the Visual Studio Code extensions and install them. Make sure your system has node and npm installed if you have not installed them. These open source packages are required.

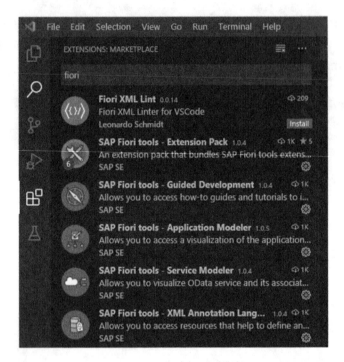

Figure 3-19. *Visual Studio Code with Fiori plug-ins*

After installing these plug-ins, developers can use Visual Studio Code to create their Fiori elements applications, as shown in Figure 3-20.

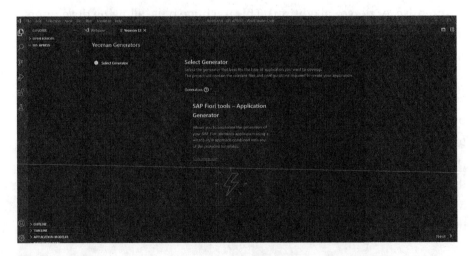

Figure 3-20. *Visual Studio Code with Fiori tools installed*

Select the *SAP Fiori Tool Generator* from the command palette (Ctrl + Shift + P) to generate an SAP Fiori application, and then select the button Next from the bottom right-hand side of Visual Studio Code.

Following the wizard, developers must select one of the available templates. In this case, the book will showcase the Worklist template from a Fiori application. Then select Next, as shown in Figure 3-21.

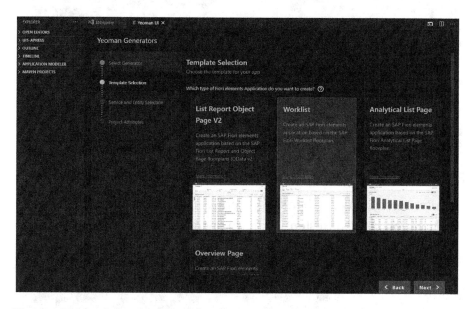

Figure 3-21. *Selecting worklist app*

After selecting the template, the developer must select the OData service (or its metadata file) that will be used to bind into the application. Since the application is not directly connected to the back-end system, the book will showcase how to import an XML metadata file as an alternative solution. From the OData service definition, get the metadata content (append /$metadata to the URL where the service is hosted) and save it as a local file into your computer. Once you save this file as metadata.xml, then select it from the data source section in the wizard, as shown in Figure 3-22. You must also select an endpoint within this OData metadata file.

Figure 3-22. *Data source configuration*

After configuring the data source, proceed to set the project configuration in the next step, as shown in Figure 3-23.

Figure 3-23. *Project configuration*

After the wizard configures all the settings, it creates the application you instructed it to create. Visual Studio Code will prompt you to open the newly created application. Agree to the prompt and open any of the files within the new Fiori application. The following package.json file is opened to show the application configuration, along with any scripts that can be executed from the CLI, and to show the project structure, dependencies, or any other setup. Notice that the UI5 application in the *Workspace* (left-hand folder hierarchy and files) shows that the *metadata.xml* file was uploaded to the **localService** folder; there is a *Component.js* and a *manifest.json* (application configuration) file.

These are very important files in all Fiori applications. Figure 3-24 has many important configuration items to observe and understand. Spend some time here to see all additional settings.

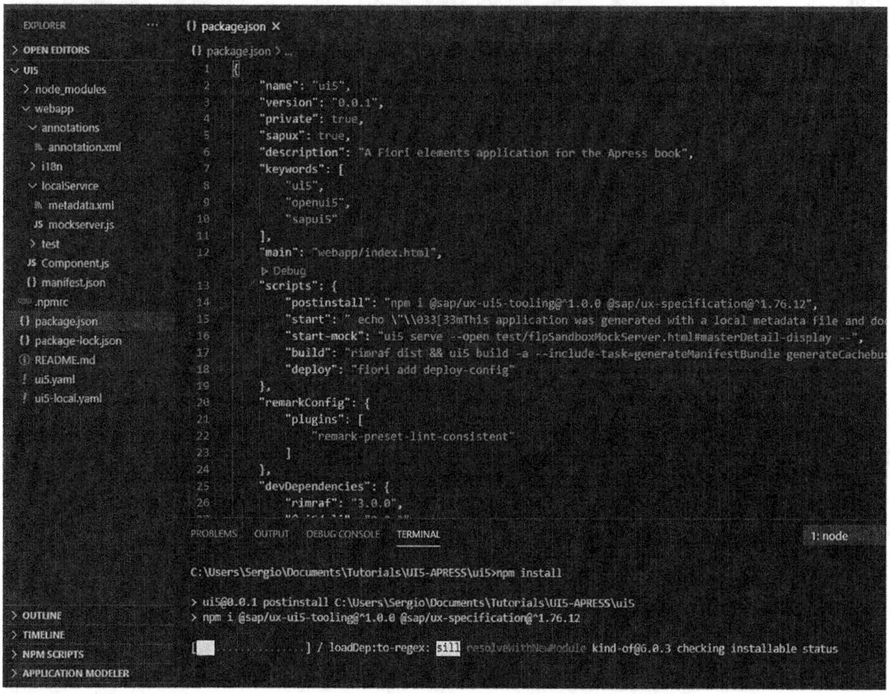

Figure 3-24. *package.json file inside Visual Code*

Once the application is ready to be shown, open the terminal window within sapui5 and first make sure all dependencies have been included. Developers may use the npm install command to run the npm command to install them. Wait until all the dependencies have been downloaded locally. Follow the npm install command with the *npm run start-mock* command, as shown in Figure 3-25. This command runs the Fiori application using the mock data since we are not directly connected to the OData service. Moreover, you can observe that the application is running a local node server and the application is served from there.

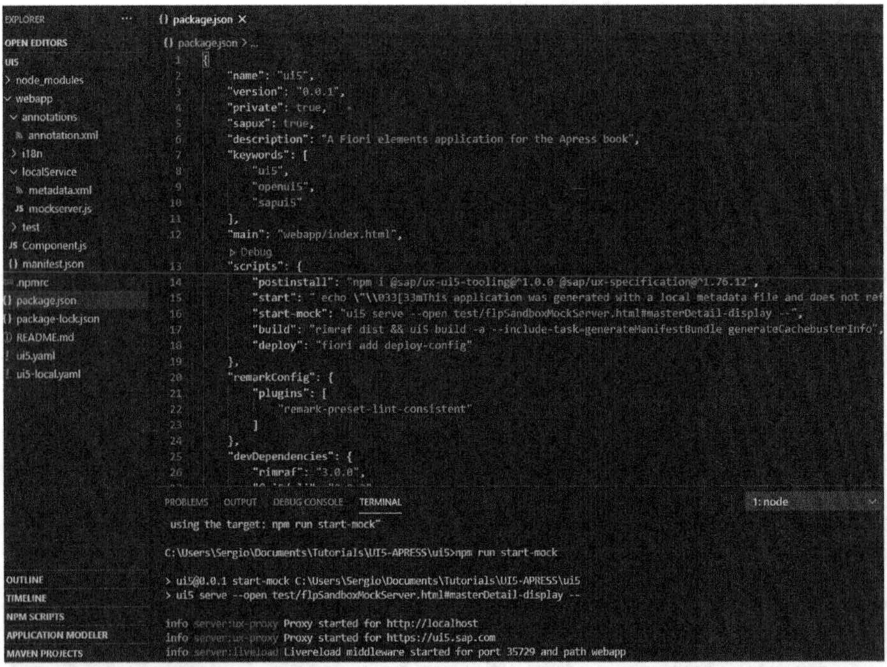

Figure 3-25. *Running npm run start-mock command*

Figure 3-26 shows the default Fiori application after the start-mock command is executed.

Initially, this application shows no data (or columns) until the developer visits the ***configuration gear icon*** located on the right-hand side of the screen. Once the pop-up opens, select the columns you wish to display. Since we selected a *Worklist* template application, the Worklist template shows the grid that we bound to the OData service, and it uses Smart controls to display the columns based on the metadata definition of our service.

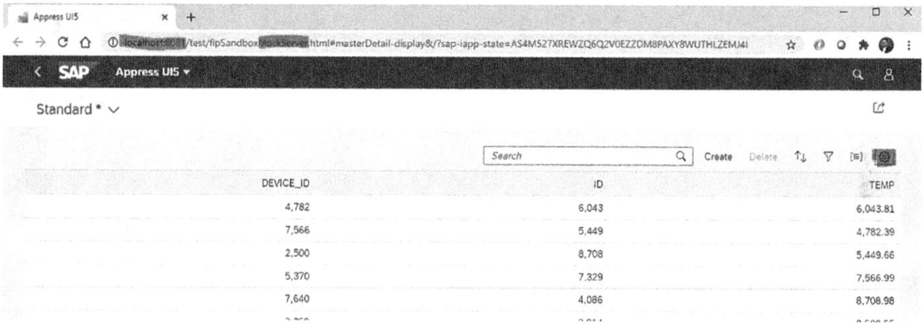

Figure 3-26. *Column configuration on Worklist template*

Row grouping is also another important feature that comes out of the box. This feature is represented by the highlighted icon in Figure 3-27. When the user selects the icon, then they must select the column to group items by. This feature is typically used when there are some repeated data on one of the columns. The following is the reflected output from selecting one of the columns to be grouped by.

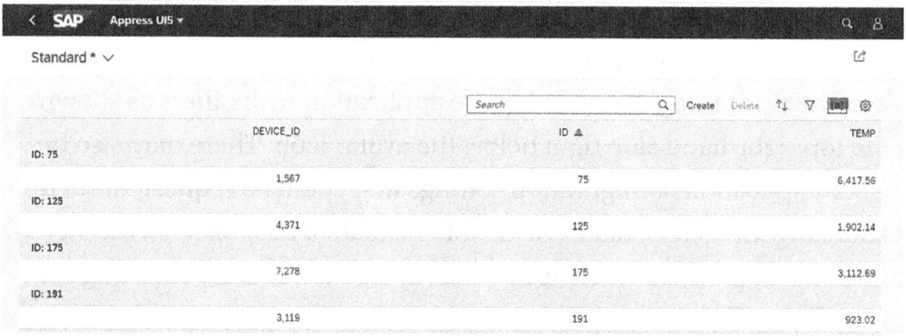

Figure 3-27. *Grouping*

105

Equally important, there are other features that come out of the box with this template, such as filtering. Select the funnel icon right next to the gear icon to see how filtering can be applied to the same Fiori application, as shown in Figure 3-28, and to its output, as shown in Figure 3-29. As mentioned before, all these features come out of the box and require not a single line of additional development efforts.

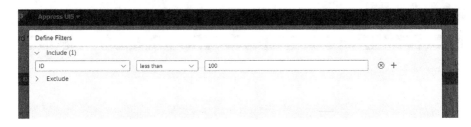

Figure 3-28. *Smart template filtering*

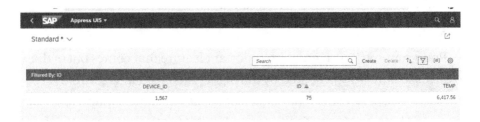

Figure 3-29. *Data output after applying filtering*

The other features such as sorting, create, and delete are there for illustration purposes; I invite you to explore them and see others such as saving the variant (showing as standard drop-down on the top left-hand side of the prior image), or sharing the application with others as shown in the top right-hand side right below the avatar icon. There may also be smaller application configuration settings that could be requested, such as changing the type of table (GridTable instead of Responsive), hiding parts of the application such as not displaying the variants, or hiding some parts of the applications; all these configuration settings are possible but somewhat tedious as the developers will be required to modify the application settings in the manifest configuration file.

By now you may be asking why in Chapter 2 we used one method of creating sapui5 applications with the SAP Web IDE, coding views, fragments, and controllers, but here in Chapter 3, the book is showing the simple approach to include the metadata definition for the same OData service and it did not require any added code. Truly, this is one of the most asked questions by many SAP customers. Usually customers even ask if coding can be skipped altogether; why would they need to use the more time-consuming approach? As everything else in software, different use cases call for different development approaches.

If you are developing for a very standard application and there is not really a need for customization, then the approach of Chapter 3 using Fiori elements is the way to go. It will save you a lot of time and development investment, but there will not be a lot of freedom for easy customization. Customization in this approach is done by modifying the manifest.json file configuration and by adding annotations in XML.

In contrast, if the application your team is trying to develop requires customization, introduction of business rules, and flexibility, and pretty much it is not going to be a standard display application, then your team/ organization needs to be thinking in terms of the customization approach shown in Chapter 2.

There are Fiori guidelines that can be followed to see which type of development is the one you and your organization need to follow. Check those Fiori guidelines in the SAP Fiori guideline web URL: `https:// experience.sap.com/fiori-design/`.

Integrating External JS Libraries into (SAPUI5) Fiori

After familiarizing ourselves with the development tools, and starting to work with one of the application tools, it is very likely that sometimes there is a need to integrate additional JavaScript libraries when the SAPUI5 library does not provide certain functionality or if there is a need to leverage other libraries with the purpose of making a more robust Fiori application. Third-party libraries are commonly included as dependencies of web applications, and in our case, the book will showcase one of them that it used in the past.

The third-party library the book would like to demonstrate is called moment.js. Moment.js is a free JavaScript library that is used for dealing with date objects. Typically, in JavaScript it is not easy or straightforward to work with date objects. There are many reasons why there may be a need to use this third-party library, including

1) Adding dates

2) Comparing dates

3) Dealing with time zones and offsets

Figure 3-30 is a picture of the moment.js website, where developers can download this third-party library.

Read the documentation and any license information to make sure your project is ok to use this library.

Figure 3-30. *Moment.js website*

To add this library into our project, first download it from their website. Then include it as a dependency. In Figure 3-31, there was a folder added called ***externalLibs***; included inside of it is the moment.js library. The dependency is injected in the detail controller file and then referenced as moment.js.

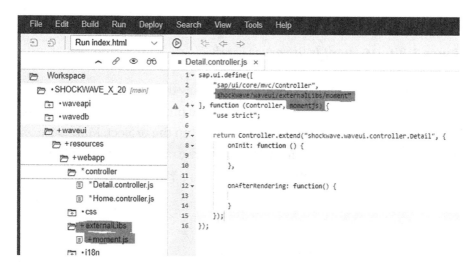

Figure 3-31. *Loading moment.js as a dependency*

Once the moment library is loaded into our project, developers may be able to reference its different operation, as shown in Figure 3-32.

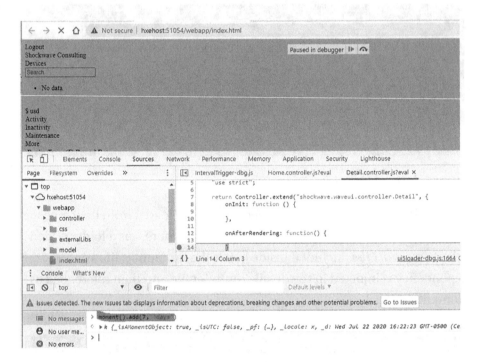

Figure 3-32. *Moment.js library is ready*

To include other third-party libraries, follow the same approach of downloading them locally, adding them to the project, and then including them as a reference to the library location within the project. Make sure you read the license terms before utilizing some of the open source libraries to avoid any potential issues.

Browser Differences, Limitations, and Features

Nowadays, the expectation when developing modern web applications is to be able to deploy our web application and have it ready to work in the different devices, browsers, and screen sizes. Most companies use Google Chrome, Mozilla Firefox, and Microsoft's Internet Explorer.

The SAPUI5 library has cross-browser support for most of its controls and templates. Next, you can observe how different browsers display the same application. There is minor visual degradation when using different browsers. Most developers and companies use Google Chrome as their preferred browser for building and using business applications; nonetheless, all major browsers should be able to display the same application with minor discrepancies between them.

Google Chrome version 83.0.4147 is shown in Figure 3-33.

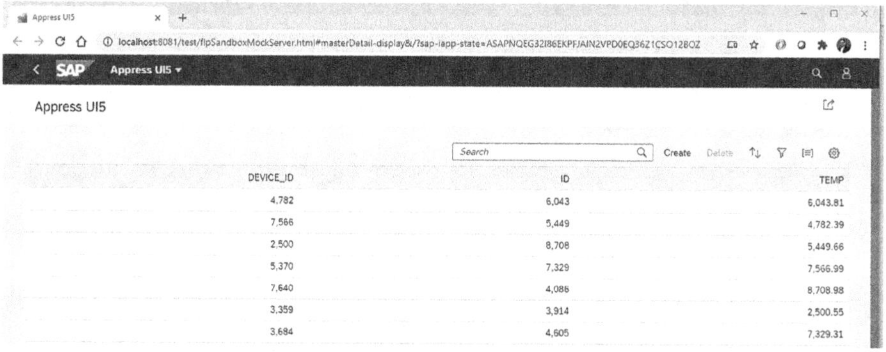

Figure 3-33. *Fiori elements List Report*

While trying to show the same Fiori elements app in the Internet Explorer browser, it errored out, saying it could not load the component file, as shown in Figure 3-34.

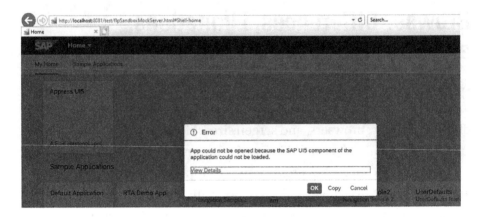

Figure 3-34. *IE shows an error due to being unable to load component*

Microsoft Edge version 83.0.478 is shown in Figure 3-35.

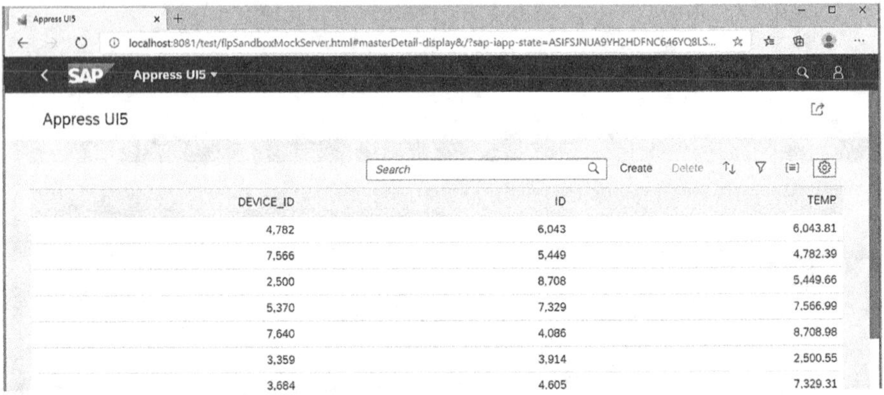

Figure 3-35. *Microsoft Edge showing the Fiori elements template for List Report*

A better comparison between these browsers would be with regard to the custom master detail application we built in SAP HANA XSA.

First, the Google Chrome browser is showcased in Figure 3-36. In my opinion, this browser shows the easiest design and is visually appealing to work with compared to Microsoft's IE and Edge browsers.

Figure 3-36. *Custom Fiori application in SAP HANA*

Secondly, the Internet Explorer browser is shown in Figure 3-37. It shows a little bit bigger font and the scroll bars are more pronounced than those seen in Google Chrome.

Figure 3-37. *Custom Fiori application in Internet Explorer*

Finally, the third browser in our comparison is the Microsoft Edge browser, and it is shown in Figure 3-38. This one seems to display fonts a little bit bigger and the different components seem to be cozier with each other.

Figure 3-38. *Custom Fiori application in Microsoft Edge*

After seeing the differences in the different browsers' renditions of
the same application, we can conclude that the visual degradations are
minor. There are sometimes non-SAPUI5 features that also are affected in
different browsers, and that is the case for JavaScript ES6 functions.

Apart from highlighting and showcasing the difference in various
browsers, the book also shows some of the debugging features that these
different browsers offer to developers.

The book shows how it accomplishes debugging in Google Chrome
version 83. To debug these SAPUI5 applications, developers can use the
browser developer tools by pressing the **F12** key on their keyboard or
by going to the browser settings – tools – developer tools, as shown in
Figure 3-39.

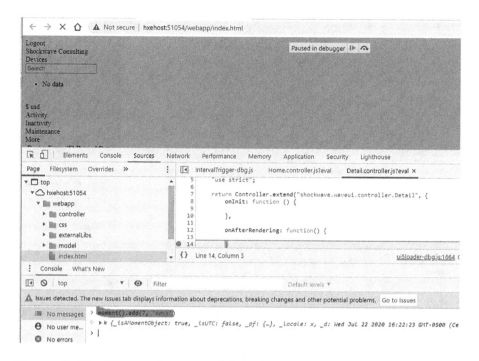

Figure 3-39. *Chrome browser debugging*

The next browser, Microsoft's Edge, uses a feature with a very similar look and feel when opening the developer tools. In fact, we can also open the developer tools using the F12 key from the keyboard. This is displayed in Figure 3-40.

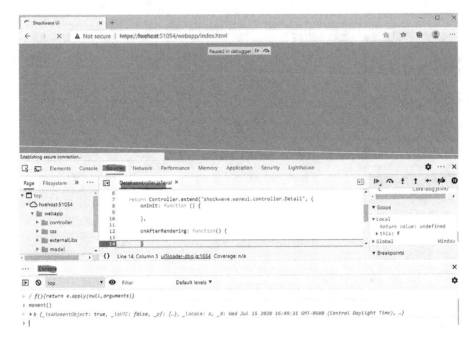

Figure 3-40. *Edge browser debugging*

Fiori Application on Various Devices

One of the featured benefits of using a framework such as SAPUI5 is that it is a responsive framework. Being responsive means that there is a single code base and the code may be able to adapt to most device screen sizes without the need to write additional custom code to make it work. As explained in Chapter 1, Fiori applications contain this feature of being responsive applications by nature. Within this section, we can observe that the SAPUI5 application we are building displays as follows in the different devices.

1) **Desktop** view – this view can be seen in all the prior images, for example Figure 3-40.

2) **Tablet** view is shown in Figure 3-41. Your browser can also simulate this view, if you open the developer tools and then select the icon device to show a responsive device. After you have selected the icon, you can also switch between tablet and other devices.

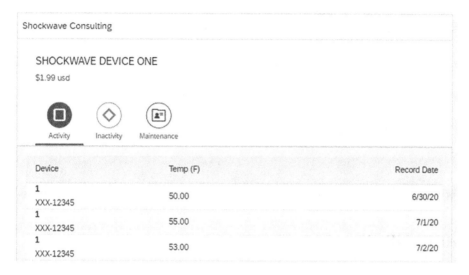

Figure 3-41. Tablet view

3) **Phone** view can be seen in Figure 3-42. This image is also shown from the browser simulator feature when opening the developer tools.

Shockwave Consulting

SHOCKWAVE DEVICE ONE

$1.99 usd

| Activity | Inactivity | Maintenance |

Device	Temp (F)	Record Date
1 XXX-12345	50.00	6/30/20
1 XXX-12345	55.00	7/1/20
1 XXX-12345	53.00	7/2/20
100		

***Figure 3-42. Phone* view**

Conclusion

Thank you for arriving at the conclusion of Chapter 3. The main purposes
of this chapter were to showcase custom applications built in SAP HANA
XSA and some of the minor possible customizations that can be done in
SAP Fiori applications that use Fiori elements. Presenting the two types
of applications was to inform you and make you aware of when to use
Fiori elements (minor to zero customizations) and also when you should
consider some of the SAP custom Fiori applications to be developed as
freestyle applications (which results in a lot more flexibility with design
and development). The chapter also touched on the various tools that can
be used while developing Fiori applications; some of these tools are open
source, some are SAP licensed. Understanding and knowing what tool to
use for the right approach will also help developers be more productive

during their development cycle. Finally, the book showed a comparison of how the same applications display differently on the different browsers and made you aware of certain performance and visual degradations while using these browsers. I hope this chapter was to your liking and that you received enough information to guide you in deciding the tools for your next development adventure.

CHAPTER 4

Unit Testing of Fiori Applications

Welcome to Chapter 4. In this chapter, the book progresses from the development stage that was shared in Chapter 3, evolving into unit testing. You may wonder if unit testing is part of development and if it needs to be accomplished by the developer. Let us start with an initial response of yes. The developer is in charge of creating a piece of software and they are indeed in charge of unit testing their code to ensure the next set of people that their development is completed and that it has no bugs. The next set of people looking at the software (with or without user interface) will naturally interact with this software and perform additional steps of testing if you will. Whether these people are intentionally trying to test the software or not, any interaction with the software is still considered testing.

If the people that are interacting with our software find an issue, then they may report it, and as a result, a bug is created and tracked with the purpose of fixing it before then releasing the software again. It becomes a cycle where the developer is constantly writing new software, adding fixes, or enhancing the original piece they created or continue to maintain. Most developers enjoy writing new software and new features – creating something new – rather than going back and fixing bugs they did not find or bugs they did not create. This chapter is to help developers with setting up their unit testing environment so that they can spend more time

© Sergio Guerrero 2021
S. Guerrero, *Custom Fiori Applications in SAP HANA*,
https://doi.org/10.1007/978-1-4842-6358-7_4

developing new features and hopefully less time doing repeated testing. That is right: one of the goals of unit testing and automating testing is to leverage tools and frameworks to set up and execute these repeated tasks, saving the developer's time and keeping the business in a continuous integration/delivery mode.

Unit Testing Frameworks

There are many ways to skin a cat, and in software development, there are many ways to perform unit testing. In this section, the book introduces a few different unit testing frameworks that have been used in prior experiences. Further, these unit testing frameworks are used in Fiori development for the user interfaces, for the consumption of OData services, and to evaluate the completeness of the application. Table 4-1 shows the different frameworks that are going to be discussed in this chapter.

Table 4-1. *Different JS Unit Test Frameworks*

Framework Name	Description	URL
QUnit	Powerful and easy-to-use JS framework	https://qunitjs.com/
Nightmare JS	High-level browser automation library	http://www.nightmarejs.org/
Puppeteer	High-level node library API to control headless Chrome dev tools	https://developers.google.com/web/tools/puppeteer

Fiori Application Unit Testing

Fiori (SAPUI5) applications use the QUnit framework just out of the box; however, other unit testing frameworks may also provide similar features to your team if you are considering other unit testing framework solutions.

Before getting into testing, developers must understand the requirement of what they are developing and what they are testing. During development, developers need to know the expected inputs and outputs they need to create meaningful and successful test cases. Understanding a unit testing scenario also requires understanding other situations of how the users will utilize their software and which devices will be used for testing.

In the first exercise, the book goes over three different test cases:

1) The first test case is to compare 1 being equal to 1 just to get us started with the framework.

2) The second test case is to compare two dates in short format.

3) The third test case contains a group of three validations (called assertions). These assertions are broken down to invoke an OData web service, to ensure the time to get data is under one second, to make sure there is at least one record being returned, and finally to compare the object structure to an expected object structure a developer has set up.

QUnit

Keeping these three test cases in mind, let us proceed to analyzing and setting up the QUnit framework in our application. The QUnit framework requires zero configuration if it will be used within the Node JS language or minimal configuration if it will be used within a browser-based application (this is our case). The reason I mentioned Node JS is because we will also use it later for some of the other frameworks. To be successful in this framework, developers must have a good handle on the JavaScript language, might well have a good understanding of the arrow functions in ES6, and should also have a good understanding of the browser developer tools.

Normally, the SAPUI5 templates contain a test folder to implement these test cases. If your project did not include such a folder, then follow the next steps to include a unit testing framework.

This first exercise will showcase the QUnit framework.

1) First, create a test folder as shown in Figure 4-1. You may include a local QUnit framework as shown in the following exercise, or if you prefer to use a Content Delivery Network resource (CDN), then you will need to reflect that URL in the script tag of the html file (line 10). In this exercise, we downloaded the QUnit framework (version 2.10.1) files from their website and included them locally in our project.

2) Next, we created a qunit.html file, shown on the right half of Figure 4-1, that will be the entry point for our unit test scenario. This file shows the output of the unit test *modules* that will be explained further. There is also a reference to the qunit-2.10.1.css file, which is used for styling the output screen of the QUnit test suite.

3) Finally, there is a reference to the test scenarios in a separate qunitTest.js file, as displayed on line 16 of Figure 4-1. It is in your best interest to modularize your unit tests so that not all your code lives in the same files. It makes life easier to have a modular approach during testing and development.

Figure 4-1. *Local QUnit framework*

After loading the external references for the QUnit scenarios, the book also references the local JQuery version 3.1.0 JavaScript file that the book will showcase to invoke a call to an OData service, and the book includes a reference to the moment.js library, as one of the exercises demonstrates the use of an external library to do formatting of the date object data type.

Double-click the test/qunitTest.js file to open it up to see the structure of the QUnit framework. In Figure 4-2, you can see the following:

a) The title given to the unit test suite, which comes from the qunitTest.html file.

b) The check boxes to hide the passed tests in case the developer only wants to display erroneous tests. Another check box to check for global settings. Finally, another check box to disable try-catch code blocks within the code.

c) The framework itself displays the number of tests completed, the time taken to complete, the breakdown of failed, passed, and skipped tests, and the total number of assertions.

d) Observing deeper into the output, the reader can also see the hierarchy output of the framework, such as

    a. ***QUnit.module*** – allows developers to group one or more test cases.

      The QUnit module accepts two arguments, the first one being the name of the module and the second one a callback function to execute its tests. There can be one or more modules within an application to separate unit tests. In Figure 4-2, the reader can see the module name highlighted (unitTestSample).

    b. ***Qunit.test*** – part of a module and can contain one or more assertions. The test section accepts two arguments: the name of the test and the function that will execute assertions within. In Figure 4-2, the reader can see the two test scenarios that exist within the same module (unitTestSample).

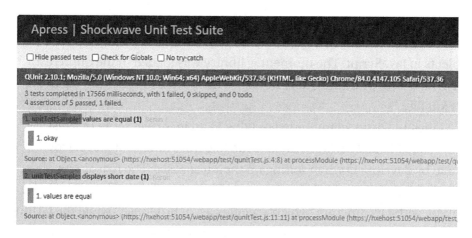

Figure 4-2. *Sample QUnit output*

Right below from each of the tests, the reader can also observe the source code and line where each test is located.

The output screen is generated from the test cases shown in Figure 4-3.

```
qunit.html  ×    ◼ qunitTest.js  ×
1⊡ QUnit.module('unitTestSample', function() {
☑ 2        var formatSmallDate = (dt) => moment().format("MM/DD/YYYY");
3
4          // simple unit test comparing two values
5 ▾        QUnit.test('values are equal', function(assert){
6              assert.equal(1,1);
7          });
8
9          // unit test ensuring the short date is formatted correctly
10 ▾       QUnit.test('displays short date', function(assert) {
11             assert.equal( formatSmallDate(new Date()), "07/29/2020", "values are equal" );
12         });
13
14 ▾       /** fails due to the async test ending before the responde of the getJSON operation
15 ▾       QUnit.test("test for calling web service and get response in less than one sec", function(assert) {
16
17             $.getJSON("/shockwaveSvc.xsodata/AVG_TEMP_DEVICES?$filter=DEVICE_ID eq 1")
18 ▾                .done(function(a){
19                     var oneSecInms = 1000;
20                     var endTime = new Date().getTime();
21                     var deltaTime = endTime - startTime;
22
23                     //****************************************************************************
24                     // fails due to the async test ending before the responde of the getJSON operation
25                     // see next test for correct implementation
26                     //****************************************************************************
27                     assert.ok(deltaTime < oneSecInms, "response took: " + deltaTime.toString() );
28                 });
29         });*/
```

Figure 4-3. *QUnit test cases*

Assertions are statements in the code to ensure the validity of what is being tested. The preceding two highlighted tests showcase a very simple test on lines 5–7 and then on lines 10–12. Notice that on line 11, the example uses a function that further uses an external library named moment. This library helps developers with the use of date and time objects in JavaScript. The moment.js library was loaded in the qunitTest. html file along with the JQuery library in the head element XML tag of the HTML file.

Lines 14–29 are commented out due to an incorrect setup of a test scenario. This section is left in the code to demonstrate a typical error made by developers when setting up their test cases. The reason this piece of code failed is that the QUnit test case was executed along with the JQuery getJSON function, which executes asynchronously, while the QUnit test section ended before reaching the success callback, resulting in an incorrect test case.

Take a deeper look into the function in Figure 4-4 to showcase the correct approach while testing an asynchronous JavaScript (AJAX) call. This QUnit test is nested within the JQuery getJSON function call.

The reason to show this test is to demonstrate the use of invoking asynchronous web services within the context of the QUnit framework to validate the following requirements:

1) The time to execute an OData call (or a REST API)

2) The asynchronous nature of web development and unit testing working together

3) Multiple assertion tests being validated within one test:

   a. Often, software must comply with Software Level Agreements (SLAs) established before the creation of a software product. In our scenario, we are testing to make sure the consumption of the OData service takes less than some agreed time to execute

b. The second assertion the book is presenting in this scenario is that the OData call contains at least one record (should not return empty array)

c. The third and last (but not least) test scenario is to validate one of the response objects with an expected object structure

```
31    var startTime = new Date().getTime();
32    // unit test to check if odata response returns in less than 1 second
33    $.getJSON("/shockwaveSvc.xsodata/AVG_TEMP_DEVICES?$filter=DEVICE_ID eq 1")
34 •      .done(function(oDataResponse){
35 •        QUnit.test("test for calling web service and get response in less than one sec", function(assert) {
36          var oneSecInms = 1000;
37          var endTime = new Date().getTime();
38          var deltaTime = endTime - startTime;
39
40          assert.ok(deltaTime < oneSecInms, "response took: " + deltaTime.toString() + " ms");
41
42          assert.ok(oDataResponse.d.results.length > 0, "there is at least 1 record in this odata call");
43
44          assert.deepEqual( Object.keys(oDataResponse.d.results[0]), ["ID","DEVICE_ID","TEMP","SERIAL_NUMBER","ENTRY_TMSTAMP"], "oData record matches required proper
45        });
46    });
47  });
```

Figure 4-4. *QUnit test using an AJAX call*

Other things to note within the third test case is that the exercise started tracking the startTime before the getJSON function (on line 31), and then it tracked the endTime right inside the success callback (on line 37) to be able to calculate the difference of time (line 38).

Figure 4-5 shows the failures that occurred when the expected object structure did not match the response from the OData service, which references the third assertion within the test case. The difference between what was expected from the OData service response and what is displayed in Figure 4-5 is the failure that the developer should understand and address.

```
3. test for calling web service and get response in less than one sec (1, 2, 3) Rerun

1. response took: 87 ms

2. there is at least 1 record in this odata call

3. oData record matches required properties
Expected:  [
                "ID",
                "DEVICE_ID",
                "TEMP",
                "SERIAL_NUMBER",
                "ENTRY_TMSTAMP"
           ]
Result:    [
                "__metadata",
                "ID",
                "DEVICE_ID",
                "TEMP",
                "SERIAL_NUMBER",
                "ENTRY_TMSTAMP"
           ]
Diff:      [
                "__metadata",
                "ID",
                "DEVICE_ID",
                "TEMP",
                "ENTRY_TMSTAMP"
           ]
Source:    at Object.<anonymous> (https://hxehost:51054/webapp/test/qunitTest.js:50:15)
           at runTest (https://hxehost:51054/webapp/test/qunit-2.10.1.js:3048:30)
           at Test.run (https://hxehost:51054/webapp/test/qunit-2.10.1.js:3034:6)
           at https://hxehost:51054/webapp/test/qunit-2.10.1.js:3265:12
           at processTaskQueue (https://hxehost:51054/webapp/test/qunit-2.10.1.js:2621:24)
           at https://hxehost:51054/webapp/test/qunit-2.10.1.js:2625:8

Source: at Object.<anonymous> (https://hxehost:51054/webapp/test/qunitTest.js:99:10) at fire (https://hxehost:51054/webapp/externalLibs/jquery-3.1.0.js:8243:31) at Object.fireWith [as resolveWith] (
(https://hxehost:51054/webapp/externalLibs/jquery-3.1.0.js:9340.9)
```

Figure 4-5. *Failure shown when expected object structure did not match the response structure from the OData service*

When writing these unit test cases, developers may also need to perform debugging of their own code.

To debug unit test cases, developers need to also look at the browser developer tools as if they were also developing a solution. To launch the developer tools, open the browser window to where the unit test HTML page is located, press F12 to launch the developer tools, and then navigate to the sources tab where the source code is located. From the sources tab, open your JavaScript file and set breakpoints to navigate through your development. Like navigating and moving around the JavaScript code, which is normally done from the controller JS file, developers can use this browser tool in the same way to help themselves navigate and debug their unit test scripts (using keyboard F10, F11, F8) or the browser navigation icons on the bottom right-hand side section.

Later in the chapter, the book will dive deeper into the Chrome developer tools, so make sure you have a good understanding of this section within the developer tools so that they will be of good use later as well.

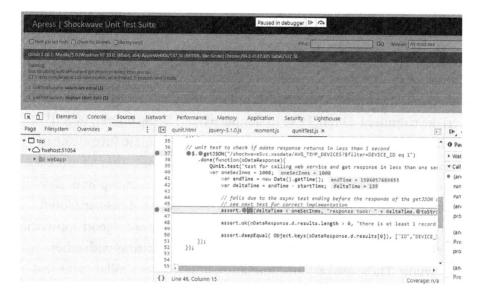

Figure 4-6. *Debugging a QUnit test case*

Learnings from this unit test framework:

1) It is very easy to set up and get started https://
   qunitjs.com/intro/

2) Documentation is easy to follow https://api.
   qunitjs.com/QUnit/

3) It is used in most Fiori application templates
   https://sapui5.hana.ondemand.com/1.36.6/docs/
   guide/e1ce1de315994a02bf162f4b3b5a9f09.html

4) Developers are familiar with most of the concepts
   used in the framework, including debugging

Spend additional time in the QUnit documentation to familiarize yourself with other types of tests, other assertions, and other operations or features offered by the QUnit framework. I wish you good luck if you decide to implement this framework!

Nightmare JS

The next unit test framework the book would like to highlight here is Nightmare JS. The reason to choose this unit testing framework is because it is a popular JavaScript framework and it is not part of the normal Fiori development. Often, I like to sample what is being offered by SAP technologies and its products, but it is also a good habit to investigate by yourself the other options available out there on the net. After all, the book is another source of information that provides different viewpoints, sharing information with the reader that may otherwise have not been explored. The result of this unit test framework is unfortunately not a good approach; however, I decided to keep it in the text to see comparisons with other frameworks. There are certain commands and features similar to the last unit framework that is documented in this chapter, and that is one of the main reasons to keep this one here, even though it yields an incomplete unit test scenario. There are some informative pieces that are relevant from the framework.

Nightmare JS is an open source high-level unit test browser automation framework. Behind the scenes, Nightmare JS uses the Electron JS framework. Electron JS (found at `https://www.electronjs.org/`) is a framework that allows developers to create cross-platform desktop apps with JavaScript, HTML, and CSS. Let me repeat that statement: cross-platform desktop apps with JS, HTML, and CSS. If you understand web development, you know that JavaScript, HTML, and CSS are languages which run on the browser and therefore are not the same as desktop applications. Electron JS is also a popular framework since web developers can now create desktop applications with familiar technologies. Having this thought in mind, let us proceed to define, explain, and showcase the Nightmare JS framework for our Fiori application unit testing as our second option.

Nightmare JS uses functions that mimic user interaction with software such as *type*, *click*, and *goto* with an API that feels synchronously, rather than having nested callbacks as done in other frameworks. Take a look at their GitHub Read Me page to learn more about this framework: `https://github.com/segmentio/nightmare/blob/master/Readme.md`

Nightmare JS can be added as a project using Node JS or it can be developed as a stand-alone unit test (Node JS) application. Following the steps from the Nightmare JS framework, install the framework from npm package using the following as the command line:

`npm install nightmare`

After running the installation command, make sure to install any dependencies using the following command line:

`npm install`

Before continuing with your unit test development, keep in mind that this framework has features that can mimic the user actions against the site; therefore, start thinking about the possible user automation of your software. There may be other frameworks that accomplish the same steps; however, I am including this one as a comparison to see how it works and what possible issues a user can face when interacting with various unit testing frameworks and also when using open source software.

The book will try to showcase the following:

1) Opening the custom application and entering credentials to authenticate

2) Verifying that the data has loaded into the master list of the application

3) Clicking an item from the list to see its details

Figure 4-7 shows the initial Nightmare JS script that demonstrates the first test scenario. Let us take a closer look at what is happening in this script.

1) Line 1 loads the nightmare js library

2) Line 7 has an object that is used for app configuration settings that are used within the script. Settings such as username, password, and home page URL belonging to this object are used within the test

3) Line 14 initializes the test

   a. Line 15 → show property allows the framework to open a window instance to show the user the automation of the entire test

   b. Line 16 passes the switches; since we do not have a secure socket layer (SSL), the exercise has to provide a flag to ignore such certification validation

   c. Line 20 opens the application using the goto command

   d. Lines 21 and 22 automate the typing of the application, setting values into the input fields with names username and password respectively

   e. Line 23 clicks the submit button (it contains the CSS class .island-button)

   f. The evaluation function invokes a function in the page and is useful to retrieve information from the page visited in the goto step

g. The then function returns a promise (line
   29) that we can see that if the user has been
   authenticated, then we are printing to the
   console displaying the username

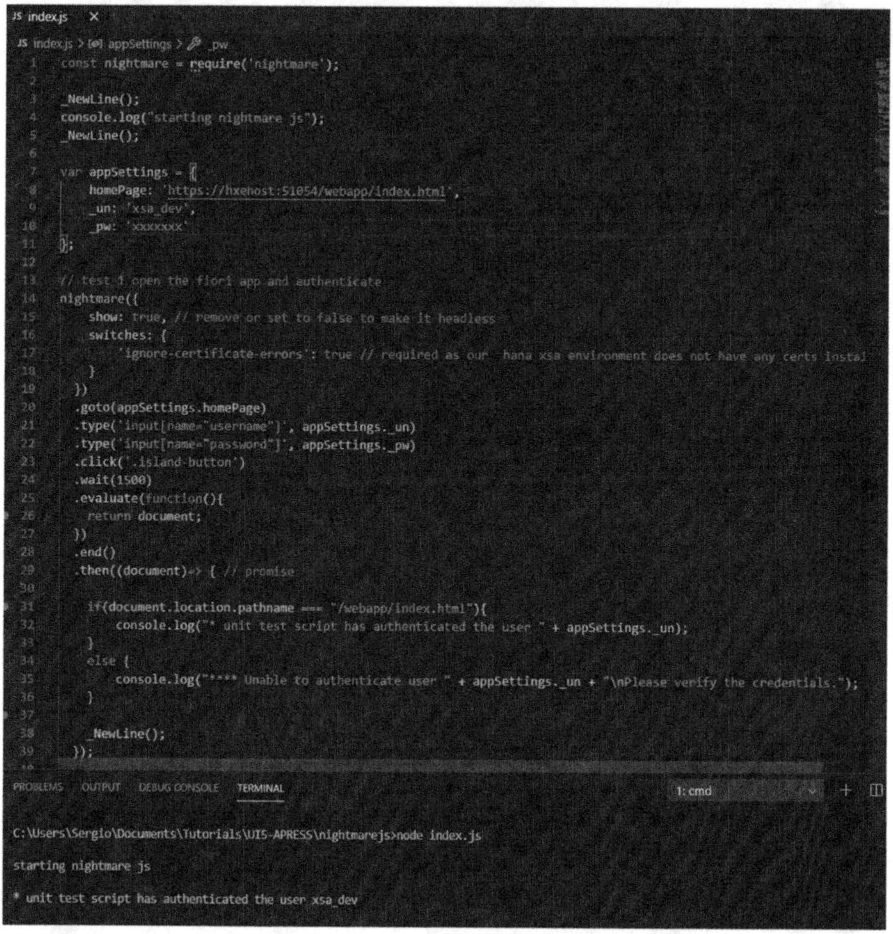

Figure 4-7. *Nightmare JS unit testing framework*

or displaying an error message if the user was unable to authenticate,
as shown in Figure 4-8 in our negative test scenario.

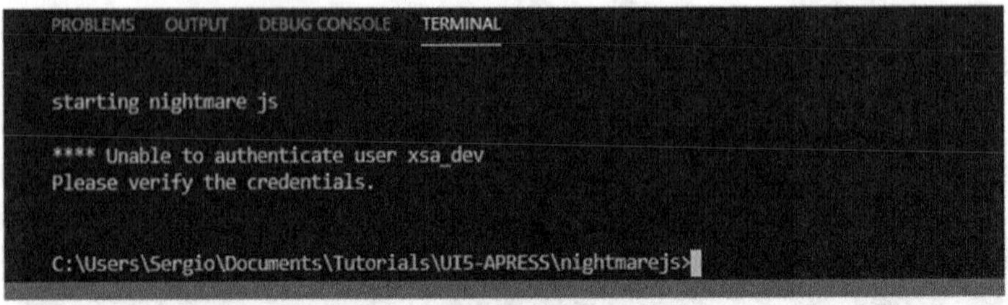

Figure 4-8. *Console output from the Nightmare JS script*

This is what the interactive window looks like when running the same test case (opens window automatically, script populates input fields, and clicks the Log On button). Notice this is not the browser window, but the window opened by Nightmare running the Electron framework in the background, as shown in Figure 4-9.

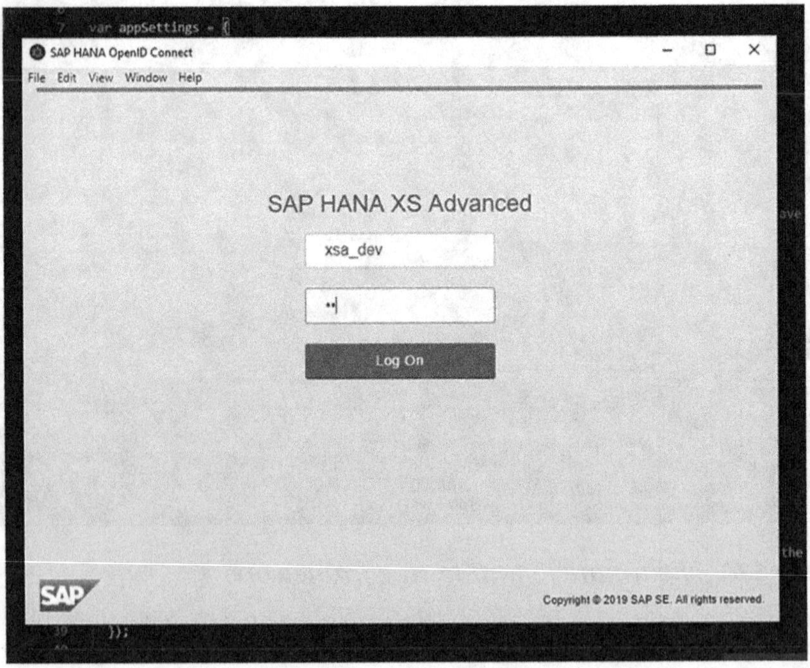

Figure 4-9. *Automated form population using Nightmare JS*

After several attempts to continue trying to use the Nightmare JS framework, I kept getting issues related to security settings. I attempted to add properties to the switch object trying to ignore these certificate errors; nonetheless, the Nightmare JS framework would not render the next step of the unit testing while running the callbacks.

Several things that I tried were to wait for the master list selector after clicking the Log On button, but that selector never rendered to the Electron window due to the fact that there were security issues with the rendering of the application. The next thing I attempted was opening the Nightmare JS application in a different user agent such as Firefox or Chrome, but because of the same security issue, the user agent would not work and the code would halt immediately. I attempted to add the developer tools to see if there were other errors coming up from the application that were preventing the framework from opening the Fiori application. I used the openDevTools setting inside the switches statement as shown in Figure 4-10.

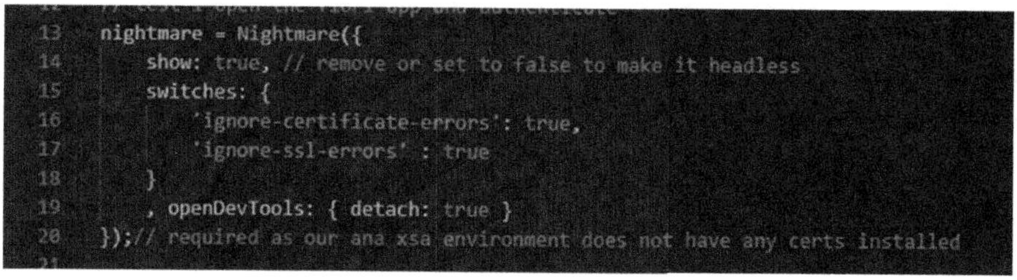

```
13   nightmare = Nightmare({
14       show: true, // remove or set to false to make it headless
15       switches: {
16           'ignore-certificate-errors': true,
17           'ignore-ssl-errors' : true
18       }
19       , openDevTools: { detach: true }
20   });// required as our ana xsa environment does not have any certs installed
21
```

Figure 4-10. *Nightmare JS switches*

This switch statement was successfully able to open the dev tools, as shown in Figure 4-11; however, the dev tools were hung on the component preload of the application and the exercise was unable to continue to use this framework, unfortunately. It was a good lesson for me as well as for other readers who are trying to evaluate various frameworks. The question becomes, at what point does a developer continue to invest time into the current framework vs. being able to move on with the evaluation and implementation of other frameworks?

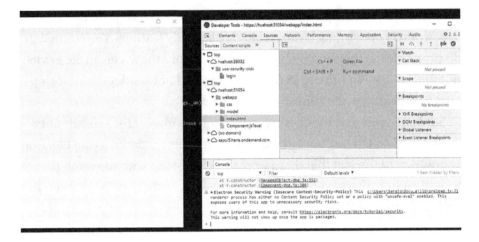

Figure 4-11. *Nightmare JS opening the devTools*

With all the previous issues and settings before from the Nightmare JS, it is now time to jump into the next unit test framework. This framework has a lot of followers and has become one of the most popular due to the proven capabilities it has. Moreover, this framework has gained acceptance due to the many available features that most developers are already familiar with while manual unit testing with their development of custom Fiori applications.

Puppeteer

Puppeteer is a great JavaScript framework developed by Google, and it is one of the best testing frameworks available now. Puppeteer uses Node JS as its JavaScript language and can be used to automate unit testing in our Fiori application and any other web application. Developers exploring this tool also need to be aware of the DOM selectors, and the common browser developer tools offered by the Google Chrome browser. The main feature of this framework is that it provides and API to control the DevTools

Protocol. Look at Figure 4-12 to see the different levels of how your Node JS script interacts with the Puppeteer API as it then interacts with the Chrome Developer Protocol (CDP) and the headless Chrome process.

Headless vs. headful? You may wonder what it means to have a headless browser. It means that the script can be automated in such a way as to not have to open the browse window. Using the CDP, the Puppeteer API can simulate everything the browser has without the need to open it. Sometimes, it is needed to use a headful browser (using a window) to see the automated interaction between the script and the browser itself. Additionally, the headful Puppeteer process can attach the browser developer tools so that the user can interact and update values at runtime.

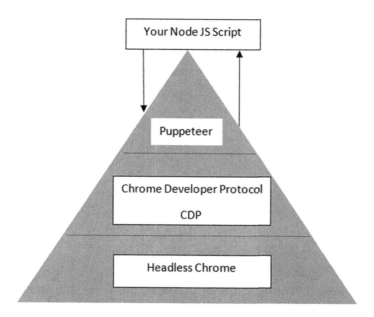

Figure 4-12. *Puppeteer architecture*

The DevTools Protocol page describes itself as follows: *"Developers can use this DevTools Protocol to inspect, interact, debug and profile Chromium, Chrome, and other Blink-based browsers."*

Earlier in this chapter, we referenced unit testing as well, the different personas validating the development, and some of the tools involved to accomplish these tasks. Most web developers are familiar with the browser tools that come up when they hit the F12 tool. Some developers have been using this tool for a while and only focus on some of the functionality to debug their code – to see when their files are being loaded during certain network requests – and some also use the browser to capture screenshots when their development is completed and validated. Capturing screenshots is sometimes required by certain processes to show that the development took place, that it was validated, and to reference how a program's code worked before and after code changes. There are other tabs within the developer tools that have additional functionality but which developers normally do not get into or that they have not had the opportunity to explore yet. With Puppeteer, these tools, their features, and their functionality are available to be interacted with programmatically.

Installing Puppeteer requires the npm command shown in Figure 4-13.

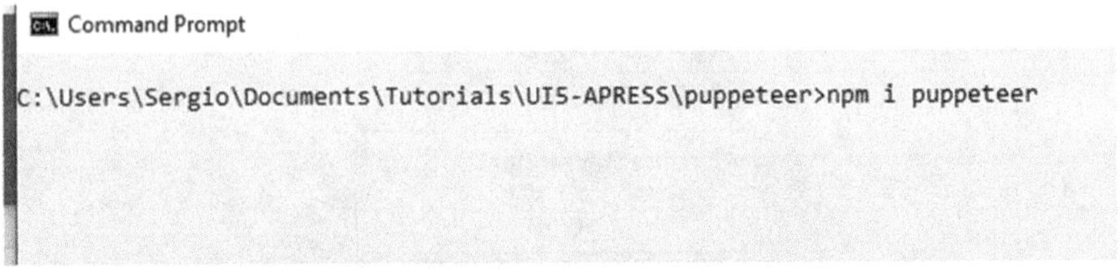

```
Command Prompt

C:\Users\Sergio\Documents\Tutorials\UI5-APRESS\puppeteer>npm i puppeteer
```

Figure 4-13. *Installing Puppeteer API using npm*

Once installed, a node script looks like Figure 4-14. This script will be used to showcase the use of Puppeteer with the custom Fiori sample application. Notice that this Puppeteer script was developed as an independent program from the custom Fiori application, and the book is showcasing the Visual Studio Code editor to develop it. This script is shown in Figure 4-14.

You might wonder why the book is using Visual Studio Code. It is because this is a free editor tool that has excellent features when developing and working with Node JS and other programming languages by enabling their corresponding extensions.

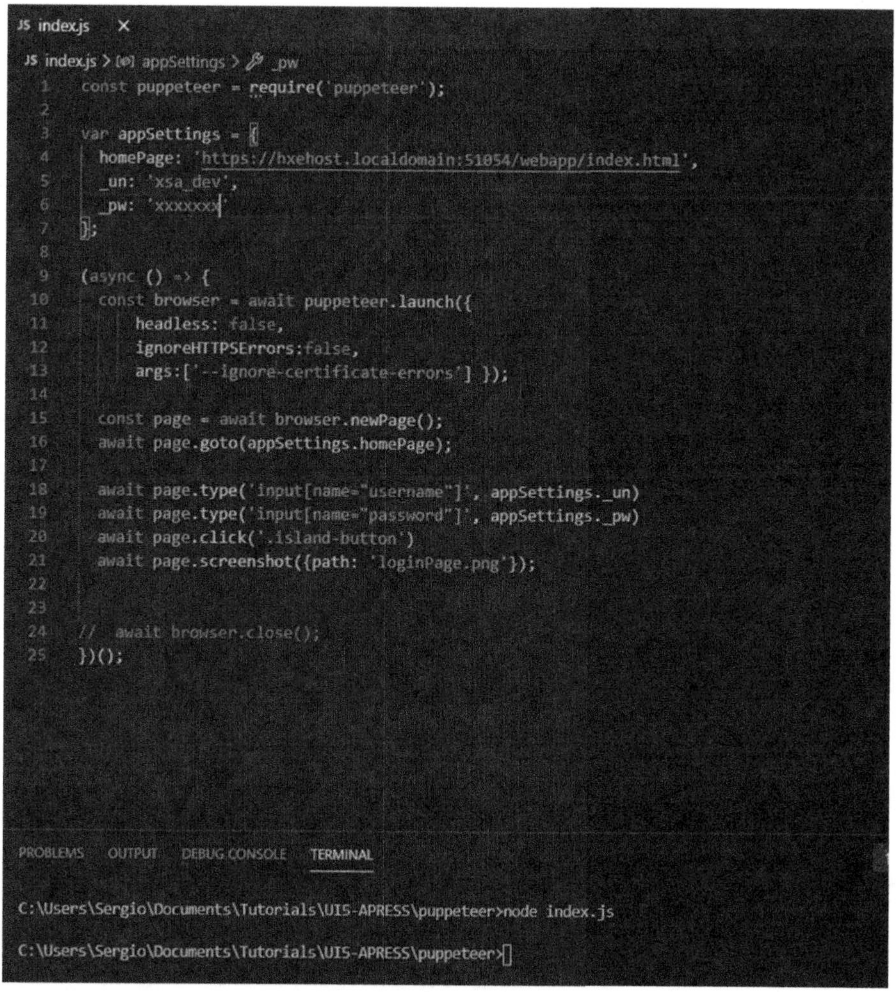
JS index.js ×
JS index.js > appSettings > _pw
const puppeteer = require('puppeteer');
var appSettings = {
homePage: 'https://hxehost.localdomain:51054/webapp/index.html',
_un: 'xsa_dev',
_pw: 'xxxxxxx'
};
(async () => {
const browser = await puppeteer.launch({
headless: false,
ignoreHTTPSErrors:false,
args:['--ignore-certificate-errors'] });
const page = await browser.newPage();
await page.goto(appSettings.homePage);
await page.type('input[name="username"]', appSettings._un)
await page.type('input[name="password"]', appSettings._pw)
await page.click('.island-button')
await page.screenshot({path: 'loginPage.png'});
// await browser.close();
})();
PROBLEMS OUTPUT DEBUG CONSOLE TERMINAL
C:\Users\Sergio\Documents\Tutorials\UI5-APRESS\puppeteer>node index.js
C:\Users\Sergio\Documents\Tutorials\UI5-APRESS\puppeteer>

Figure 4-14. *Sample Puppeteer script*

Moreover, I am pleased to announce how easy it is to work with the Puppeteer framework. It was much easier than working with the other frameworks presented in this chapter. There is a great amount of documentation on the Puppeteer site, which is found at the following URL: `https://devdocs.io/puppeteer/` as well as in other sources investigated during the writing of the book such as YouTube videos and Google searches, just to mention a few.

Now, let us explore what this preceding script has and what it does.

1) Line 1 loads the Puppeteer Node JS library (after it was installed)

2) Lines 3–5 are for the application configuration. For the simplicity of the exercise it is included in the same script; however, it can be refactored or read from a different file

3) Line 9 and below contain the main function that it is being unit tested against

   a. Notice the framework uses asynchronous programming from the entry point of view; therefore, you will also notice the await keyword on the following lines of code.

   b. Line 10 initializes a new instance of the Puppeteer framework and launches it using a few default settings, such as launching it head**ful** (headless: false), ignoring the HTTPS errors (due to a missing certificate).

   c. Since our custom Fiori application has route authentication enabled, the exercise starts by opening the homepage of the application and it must authenticate to open the application itself, as shown in Figure 4-15.

    d. The headless: false flag is used to visualize the
       application in action, as shown in Figure 4-15.
       Notice within the browser window that opened,
       right before the address bar, there is a message
       that reads *"Chrome is being controlled by
       automated test software"*, which means it is truly
       running from our script.

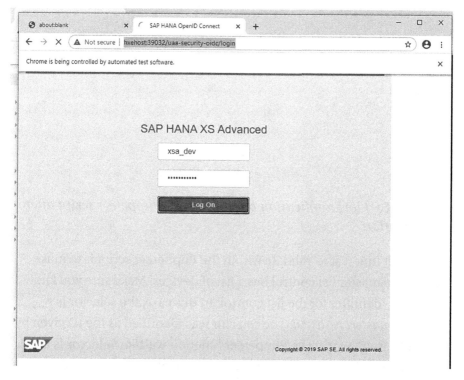

Figure 4-15. *Headful Puppeteer script launching the Fiori application*

Right after the script opens the headful browser, types the username
and password, and clicks the Log On button, the application itself redirects
to the custom Fiori application, as seen in Figure 4-16.

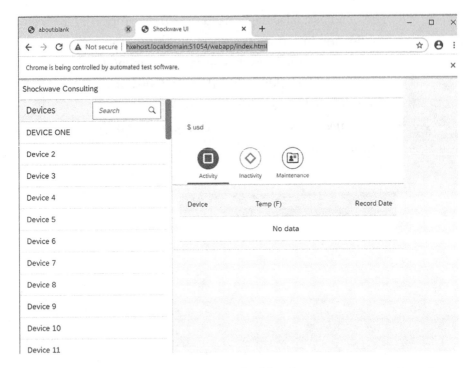

Figure 4-16. *Fiori application opened by the Puppeteer script after authentication*

The next unit test to validate within the Puppeteer script is to make sure that the master list control has a list of devices. Make sure you know the selector identifier for the list control. In this case, the selector is #__ *xmlview1--masterList-listUl*. The selector was identified as the ID given by the SAPUI5 framework. The Puppeteer function **waitForSelector** is used to provide the selector we identified in our appSettings.masterListSelector, and it was passed to the function. Inside the callback function, we simply displayed the resulting element into the console to make sure the item existed. If you are curious about what other properties exist inside the callback, set a breakpoint inside the script before invoking the waitForSelector function and inside the **then** callback to inspect these objects. Look at Figure 4-17 to learn more about the implementation to wait for the selector and then running an investigation of it.

```
JS index.js  ×
JS index.js > [∅] appSettings
    1    const puppeteer = require('puppeteer');
    2
    3  > var appSettings = {
    8    };
    9
   10    (async () => {
   11        const browser = await puppeteer.launch({
   12            headless: false,
   13            ignoreHTTPSErrors:false,
   14            args:['--ignore-certificate-errors'] });
   15
   16        const page = await browser.newPage();
   17        await page.goto(appSettings.homePage);
   18
   19        await page.type('input[name="username"]', appSettings._un)
   20        await page.type('input[name="password"]', appSettings._pw)
   21        await page.click('.island-button')
   22        await page.screenshot({path: 'loginPage.png'});
   23
   24        // once in the home page, wait for the list to show up
   25        await page.waitForSelector(appSettings.masterListSelector)
   26            .then((element) => {
   27                console.log('master list selector exists : ' + element._remoteObject.description); });
   28
```

Figure 4-17. Puppeteer script waiting for selector

The next unit test to validate within the Puppeteer script is to make sure that clicking a device list item will populate the details view (right-hand side of the screen). This test is very powerful because we are mimicking the user interaction between the displaying of the app and the user clicking a list item to see its details. The tricky part here is to understand that the list may have 1, 2, or 100 items in it and we want to make sure we can select not only the first one but any of the list items in the list. My first thought was to select the children on the list and get the nth child based on JQuery rules or some selector. Then, I let my brain work a little bit more and I remembered that the JavaScript language has a random function in its Math library. I went ahead and included a variable to obtain a random number between 0 and the length of the list items. Once the random number was identified, then we needed to click such an element – yes!!! It sounds extremely good thinking it out loud, but the next hurdle is to get the random item from the list and then somehow click it.

In Figure 4-18, you can observe the new function I added to let the Puppeteer framework wait for the selector based on the element, ul, which is an unordered list, and the list item, li, based on an assigned CSS class. This CSS class is one provided by the SAPUI5 framework, and I was able to obtain it by opening the dev tools and identifying it.

After the Puppeteer framework waits for the list items, these items are passed to the callback function for further investigation to see how many records exist, for example. The next thing I did was to display into the console the first item from these list items.

Then, I calculated the random value I described before and I used the return key because I wanted to use this element into my next callback, where I added the click function based on the returned element from the current callback function. It is amazing how the framework really allows asynchronous operations on these elements, plus it also allows the chaining of the elements as we identify and calculate one scenario and can pass it into the next for further investigation and profiling.

I suggest you carefully examine Figure 4-18 a few times to see how all the JavaScript concepts play well in this framework.

```
JS index.js   ×

JS index.js >  <function> >  then() callback
1     const puppeteer = require('puppeteer');
2
3   > var appSettings = {
8     };
9
10    (async () => {
11        const browser = await puppeteer.launch({
12            headless: false,
13            ignoreHTTPSErrors:false,
14            args:['--ignore-certificate-errors'] });
15
16        const page = await browser.newPage();
17        await page.goto(appSettings.homePage);
18
19        await page.type('input[name="username"]', appSettings._un)
20        await page.type('input[name="password"]', appSettings._pw)
21        await page.click('.isIsland-button')
22        await page.screenshot({path: 'loginPage.png'});
23
24        // once in the home page, wait for the list to show up
25        await page.waitForSelector(appSettings.masterListSelector)
26  >           .then((element) => {
28               });
29
30        // $$ using the Puppeteer API
31        await page.$$('ul > li.sapMLIB')
32            .then((listItems) => {
33                console.log("number of list items : ", listItems.length);
34
35                if (listItems.length>0) {
36                    console.log("First list item : ", listItems[0]._remoteObject.description);
37                }
38
39                // get a random item
40                var randomIndex = Math.floor(Math.random() * (listItems.length + 1));
41                console.log("selecting item " + randomIndex.toString());
42                return listItems[randomIndex];
43            })
44            .then((element) => {
45                console.log("item was clicked and details are set");
46                element.click();
47            });
```

Figure 4-18. *Puppeteer script waiting on a selector, calculating a random value, and clicking a list item*

The next screenshot, Figure 4-19, is displayed to show the readers the powerful things that can be accomplished in a scripted way, but also we can see them in the real window as if a user would be performing this interaction with our custom Fiori application.

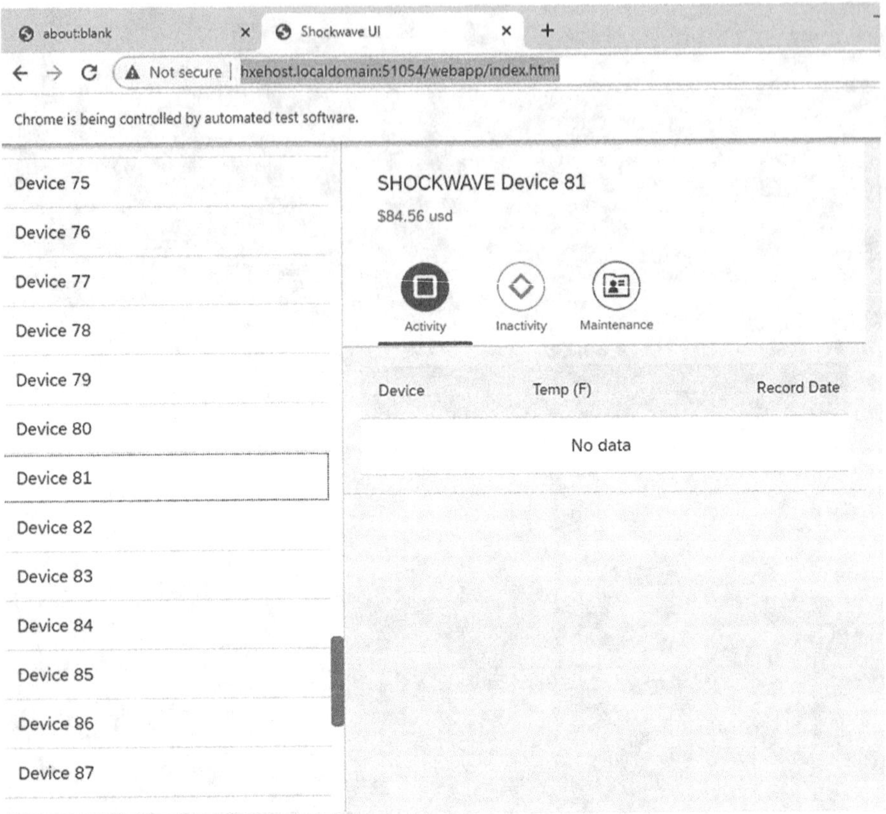

Figure 4-19. *Puppeteer script selecting random list item to display its details*

For the purpose of the reader, the Visual Studio Code console looks like this after having run the preceding scenario, and it is shown in Figure 4-20.

Figure 4-20. *Console output from Puppeteer script*

Last but not least, we can script the Puppeteer unit test to close itself when it has completed by uncommenting the line await browser.close() at the end of the main function, as shown in Figure 4-21.

```js
JS index.js    ✕
JS index.js > ⦿ <function>
 1    const puppeteer = require('puppeteer');
 2
 3  > var appSettings = {
 8    };
 9
10    (async () => {
11        const browser = await puppeteer.launch({
12            headless: false,
13            ignoreHTTPSErrors:false,
14            args:['--ignore-certificate-errors'] });
15
16        const page = await browser.newPage();
17        await page.goto(appSettings.homePage);
18
19        await page.type('input[name="username"]', appSettings._un)
20        await page.type('input[name="password"]', appSettings._pw)
21        await page.click('.island-button')
22        await page.screenshot({path: 'loginPage.png'});
23
24        // once in the home page, wait for the list to show up
25        await page.waitForSelector(appSettings.masterListSelector)
26  >             .then((element) => {
28                });
29
30        // $$ using the Puppeteer API
31        await page.$$('ul > li.sapMLIB')
32  >             .then((listItems) => {
43                })
44  >             .then((element) => {
47                });
48
49    await browser.close();
50    })();
```

Figure 4-21. *Closing browser at the end of the Puppeteer script*

This time the script was run, and it quickly opened the window, ran the different scenarios, and closed itself at the end of execution. In Figure 4-22, we can see the log of the unit test, but the human factor was not able to capture the screenshot during the quick run of the script.

Figure 4-22. Final console output after running entire script

So far we have run several unit test cases using the Puppeteer framework to show the user interaction with the software; however, none of the test scenarios showed the network requests nor the data being transferred from the app to the OData service and vice versa.

I will proceed to include one of these tests so that we can have a more complete unit test framework; it is also part of the automated script we are writing. At the end of the day, we need to also validate the data being sent back and forth from the application with a back-end system. Without further ado, here it is. Let us temporarily remove the browser close command so that we can allow the application to do the interception and analysis of the API request/response before closing the headful browser window, as shown in Figure 4-23.

Developers can observe the Puppeteer script showing the following:

1) page.on ('request', InterceptedRequest =>

   This callback allows the developer to analyze the request before it is sent to the back-end API. Developers can see current values, edit request headers, and request parameters and any other setting related to the HTTP(s) request.

2) page.on('response', InterceptResponse =>

This callback allows developers to analyze the response object, including the response, headers, cookies, and response actual data, among any other setting you can think of when receiving an HTTP(s) response object.

For simplicity of the exercise, the Puppeteer script is also doing a few console.log statements so that developers can see those values during their unit testing as shown in Figure 4-23.

Should any developer wish to see other values in the callback, they can also hover over the request/response variables to analyze those properties or also type in the debugging console to view the runtime values of specific objects.

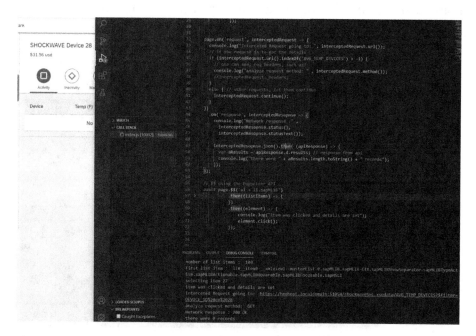

Figure 4-23. *Puppeteer script intercepting network request and response*

Earlier in the book, we introduced a function to generate a random index as the selection of the master list control. Let us now interact with the custom Fiori application and make a manual selection from the current Puppeteer window to select a record which has additional records in the API request that is being intercepted. That's right: the headful session can also be interacted by the user while performing the unit test of the application.

In Figure 4-24, the user has manually selected the DEVICE ONE record from the master list, and you can observe on the background application (left side of the image with white background) that the details of the item selected are displayed in the application while the Visual Code console (right side of Figure 4-24 in black background) is also showing the intercepted request where the request method was logged (GET), as well as the intercepted response (status 200 OK and seven records being returned, of which only five contain the Activity, which moreover are the records being displayed under the Activity tab of the application).

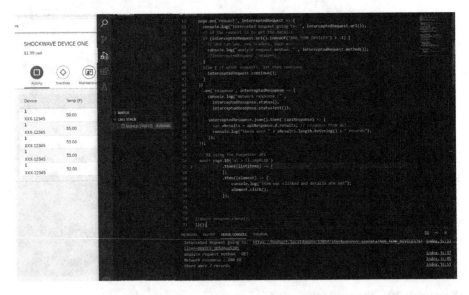

Figure 4-24. *Manually selected list item to analyze the intercepted response object*

Thus, the Puppeteer exercise concludes; I truly believe this framework has added great advantages and benefits to our unit testing chapter. Starting from the QUnit framework, which is very close to our application and nicely integrates with the SAPUI5 framework, most developers will probably feel comfortable without needing to do any additional setup or configuration, which sometimes can be overwhelming or too time consuming, such as what occurred with the Nightmare JS framework in my instance. Moving on to the Puppeteer framework, I found this framework to have some advanced features while being extremely well documented in most of the online resources that I have researched or stumbled upon when building various test cases. I would gladly and highly recommend Puppeteer to anyone doing web development, because it is such a clean and easy-to-use framework that covers most if not all of the possible test cases that developers need to test doing their software development; anything from being able to authenticate users by typing usernames and passwords, to being able to trigger click events into buttons or links, to intercepting the http(s) requests when loading or posting data. This framework has truly gained my vote as the best unit testing framework, and I am glad that I can use it as an external option while building and validating custom Fiori applications. The options to use headful and headless features are extremely important if the users require seeing what is happening during their test. Once they feel comfortable with their development, they can choose to minimize processing by going headless in their unit testing scripts. Hats off to the Puppeteer team for such a slick product.

Improvements Resulting from Unit Testing

Unit testing is beneficial when developing software applications; however, for developers there should be more than just being able to prove their work is correct. Developers sometimes find this type of task to be tedious and customers sometimes think this is an unnecessary expense. In this section, the book will showcase a few scenarios that have proven the previous assumptions to be wrong.

1) How does unit testing make my code better?

Understanding a task and being able to test it out allows the developer to showcase his/her work as per the requirement. Writing unit tests allows developers to double-check their own work programmatically in case it needs to be updated several times due to a change in requirement or enhancement of the software product. Developers get better and better at their craft if they not only develop their requirements but understand the testing scenarios their software must be submitted to. In addition, automation of one's work is crucial to inject different test values, such as the one presented in the Puppeteer example, where generation of a random number was utilized to trigger a read of an API operation to retrieve the details linked to a list item.

2) How does unit testing save my project time?

There are situations where a software product needs to be built in incremental phases. Nowadays, most companies are following an Agile methodology, and software products evolve after many iterations and feedback from their business users. Having a scripted unit test framework at hand will reduce the time to deliver these enhancements and the necessary time to validate new software additions or changes. Eliminating the human factor to run these unit tests is one way to save overall time and make the project more robust when these changes/integrations are introduced. Moreover, if we have several pieces of our software following these unit test frameworks, then we can also automate our testing to minimize time after development and after deployment, as most companies do during integration and regression testing.

3) How does my unit testing generate improvements to my software?

Improvements in performance can be demonstrated in different ways:

a) Performance when starting an application

b) Performance when loading (MVC) views

c) Performance when accessing external resources such as images or other scripts

d) Performance when loading data from a web service

Keep in mind that the initial overhead of creating unit testing scripts requires some extra time at the beginning of a software project, while additional enhancements to the same software product can leverage these test case scenarios, making development and its integration with other systems more robust in the long run.

Additional improvements resulting from experience in other custom Fiori applications include but are not limited to the following:

1) Setting the sapui5 application to load asynchronously, as shown in Figure 4-25.

```
/ork    Performance    Memory    Application    Security    Lighthouse

[◄]   index.html ×   IntervalTrigger-dbg.js   Home.controller.js?eval   Detail.controller.js?eval

 1  <!DOCTYPE HTML> ▲
 2  <html>
 3
 4    <head>
 5        <meta http-equiv="X-UA-Compatible" content="IE=edge" />
 6        <meta charset="UTF-8">
 7        <title>Shockwave UI</title>
 8        <script id="sap-ui-bootstrap"
 9            src="https://sapui5.hana.ondemand.com/resources/sap-ui-core.js"
10            data-sap-ui-libs="sap.m"
11            data-sap-ui-theme="sap_fiori_3"
12            data-sap-ui-compatVersion="edge"
13            data-sap-ui-preload="async"
14            data-sap-ui-resourceroots='{"shockwave.waveui": "./"}'>
15        </script>
16        <link rel="stylesheet" type="text/css" href="css/style.css">
17        <script>
```

Figure 4-25. *Asynchronously bootstrapping sapui5*

You can also observe this in the Network tab to
visualize the resources being loaded, as also shown
in Figure 4-26.

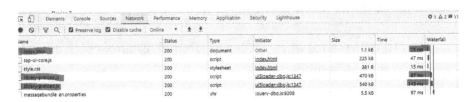

Figure 4-26. *Network tab showing the preloaded resources*

2) Minifying JavaScript files to improve application
    load performance (make sure your files run through
    a minification process; their extension names could
    be *.min.js). The minification process can also be
    applied to style sheet files. In the exercise presented
    in this book, there are two js libraries being used:
    the jquery library and the moment.js library. Both
    are minified and shown in Figure 4-27.

⊞ • css

🗁 • externalLibs

📄 • jquery-3.1.0.js

📄 • moment.js

Figure 4-27. *Minified external libraries*

3) If your custom application uses image files, make
   sure the images are of good quality and their size
   can quickly be read and loaded into the application.
   Running your browser developer tools to see the time
   to load these images can improve your loading time.

4) Utilize sap icons for some of the actions that are
   required in your application. Since the icons
   provided by the SAPUI5 framework are already part
   of the same library, you can take advantage of using
   these icons. Moreover, using these icons such as
   the ones included in the icon tab bar of the exercise
   also benefits your Fiori development, since you are
   including resources that are within the rules and
   guidelines of the framework.

5) Improvements while loading data from OData
   services include being able to set up the SAPUI5
   control aggregator to load such data on demand
   and also to include a number of visible elements
   as a threshold, resulting in the control only loading
   what is needed or what is visible for the end user.
   Following this advice has truly made our custom
   Fiori applications have the look and feel of modern
   and fast web applications, as shown in Figures 4-28
   and 4-29.

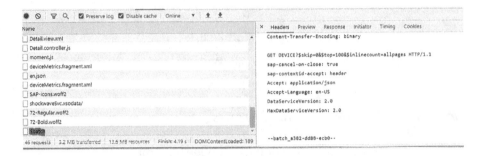

Figure 4-28. *OData service making batch requests*

Figure 4-29. *Async resource loading*

Conclusion

As I arrive to the end of this chapter, there is a bittersweet memory of the experiences I want to share with all the readers; there are some development frameworks (for unit testing and for non-unit testing) which require simple configuration, and sometimes there may be a lot of more advanced and deeper technical knowledge required when using these frameworks. I suggest that all developers become familiar with a couple of choices before deciding on which framework they are willing to implement, study, and run with. There are other factors in our projects that may limit us from time and resources and those extra factors are the main reasons why projects sometimes end up with simple unit testing frameworks, while other times they end up with more elegant solutions, as I have discovered Puppeteer to be one of the most elegant and simple solutions currently available.

Analyzing pros and cons for each framework should be part of your unit test design. Further, looking at the available documentation should be a driving factor to adopt a framework when developers are getting into newer territory. I found Puppeteer to be my favorite choice of unit testing framework, even though I only touched on the surface of the framework due to limitations on space and time for the writing of this text. I hope you can use some of the scripts shared during the exercise to get into or expand your knowledge of the unit testing frameworks. Last but not least, there are other manual alternatives for you to get started into unit testing if you are still not comfortable with automated testing; we all start somewhere and I hope you can master the manual steps first and then get into one of these enterprise-level reputable options. I cannot wait to hear feedback from you if you decide to expand on QUnit, Nightmare JS, or Puppeteer. I wish you good luck in your implementation!

CHAPTER 5

Deploying Custom Fiori Applications

Welcome to the final chapter of *Custom Fiori Applications*. This is an exciting chapter because everything that has been presented thus far is now going to be promoted to a different environment so that it can be used by people other than developers. Deploying an application involves more than copying files or clicking buttons to make our software move from a local workspace or development environment into a quality environment or, even better, eventually into a production environment. There is probably a set of items that need to be verified before software is deployed to upstream environments. Depending on the company's policies, certain steps may be followed during the software development life cycle, including related steps to approve and release software. There may be certain nontechnical requirements that need to be met prior to the release of this or other web applications.

The book assumes that pre-requirements have been met – documentation updated, quality assurance (QA) testing met, user acceptance testing (UAT) completed, and approvals from managers received – before the next set of steps is executed. Also, any external accounts used are already created in the SAP Cloud Platform or the Amazon Web Service (AWS) environments.

© Sergio Guerrero 2021
S. Guerrero, *Custom Fiori Applications in SAP HANA,*
https://doi.org/10.1007/978-1-4842-6358-7_5

Preparing the Deployment and Software Versioning

When preparing and releasing software, there are various places where versioning can be tracked for the application itself and for auditing purposes. As developers and technical owners of software, we also must keep track of the different integration points we have with other external software libraries. Within this custom Fiori application, the book used the versions shown in Table 5-1.

Table 5-1. *Software Versions Used during the Development of the Fiori Application*

Software or library	Version	How to figure out version
HANA XSA	HANA 2 SPS 04	HANA XSA installation
Fiori UX	3	Configured in index.html
SAPUI5	1.80.1	Ctrl + Shift + Alt + P from browser
Node JS	12.16.1	cmd node -v from cmd line
NPM	6.13.4	cmd npm -v from cmd line
JQuery	3.1.0	Open file from IDE
Moment.JS	2.27.0	Open file from IDE
QUnit	2.10.1	Open file from IDE
Nightmare JS	3.0.2	node_module from IDE
Puppeteer JS	5.2.1	node_module from IDE
OData	v2 and v4	Metadata of the file from browser
mta.yaml	0.0.1	Configured by developer from SAP Web IDE

As you can see, there are many integrations in the example custom Fiori application, and they need to be looked at and maintained while making sure that whatever it is developed with, is also maintained when it reaches the production environment. Keeping software versioning handy is extremely important when issues and bugs are reported due to issues that may not be part of a feature implemented by the Fiori developer; sometimes, these issues may arise from a dependency of these external libraries or modules. Often, companies may conduct audits against a company that follows compliance processes, and it is always very useful to have proof of documentation for such situations.

You may wonder what other reasons are required to keep the versioning available when developing custom Fiori applications. Generally, there can also be new releases of the external dependencies, and in that situation, developers may need to consult their documentation and logs to verify which versions they currently have and to see if it is worth upgrading to a newer release or if the newer release is compatible with the rest of their environment. There are general guidelines when software is generally available and from time to time, newer features may even require newer hardware. Sometimes, there are minor releases or even patches in software that may not have a huge impact in the development and integration of custom applications; in such situations, there may be little to no impact and the integration may be safe to adopt. If the upgrade of a dependency is coming in the form of a major release, then it is advisable to analyze the impact of the new features, pros/cons, and what benefits are being offered to understand if it makes sense to plan for an upgrade. This is a common scenario with SAP software or other paid software that goes through a release cycle providing its customers with the latest and greatest features available.

As displayed in Table 5-1, software comes in a variety of versions. Best practices in software versioning describe the version pattern as X.Y.Z, where

1) **X** represents a major release number. A major release means that various features were added to the software and released.

2) **Y** represents a minor release number. A minor release means that a small feature was added to the software and released.

3) **Z** represents a patch number. A patch number means that a different build of the software was added and released.

If you are wondering how to maintain our custom Fiori application, then look at the mta.yaml file, which is part of the SAPUI5 module inside the Fiori project in the SAP Web IDE. Open the SAP Web IDE, navigate to the project, open the UI5 module named waveui, and then double-click the mta.yaml file, as shown in Figure 5-1.

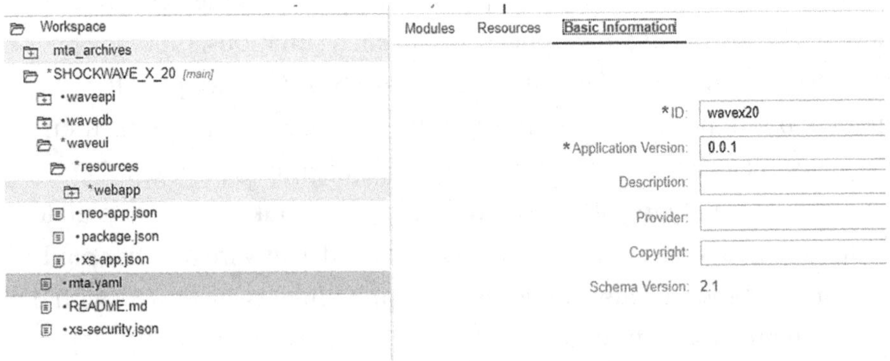

Figure 5-1. *mta.yaml version*

In this image, the reader can observe that the *application version* is identified as 0.0.1; that means that this is the initial version of the software being developed. The next question the developer needs to raise is how the version of this piece of work increments as new features are added or the product evolves over its lifetime. That is done in the mta.yaml file by increasing the 0.0.1 version to 0.0.2, 0.0.3, and so on, as shown in Figure 5-2. This mta yaml file only exists if the development occurs in the XSA environment, which follows the Cloud Foundry (CF) principles. Be aware that this development artifact (file) does not exist in the XS classic version of SAPUI5 applications.

Figure 5-2. *Building the project to generate an mtar file*

The result of running the build process at the project level creates an mtar file (MTA = Multi-Targeted Application archive), which is the main file that is used to deploy software from the SAP Web IDE to the targeted environment, as shown in Figure 5-3. This is a binary file and it is used for deployment purposes only.

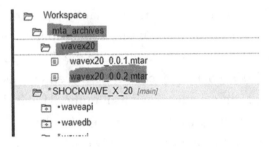

Figure 5-3. *mtar generated files*

The SAP Web IDE has functionality to be able to deploy this development code (mtar file) by selecting it and then selecting the Deploy menu from the SAP Web IDE, as shown in Figure 5-4. Once the Deploy menu is selected, then developers can choose if they will deploy to the SAP Cloud Platform, or to the XS Advanced environment (on premise), as shown in Figure 5-4. Toward the end of the chapter, there will be a similar exercise running the same tool, SAP Web IDE; however, it will be used to deploy into Amazon Web Services (AWS).

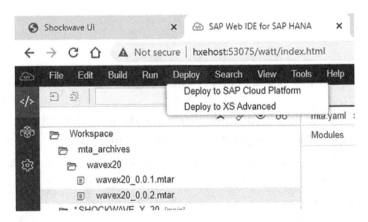

Figure 5-4. *Selecting a target environment to deploy the Fiori application*

Deploying to an on-premise XS Advanced environment is shown in the following to see how the development instance (identified by a unique identifier and also the name of the sapui5 module waveui) is shown alongside of the released instance identified by its module name waveui in Figure 5-5.

⌂ Home / 🔒 HANAExpress / 🖥 development ⌄

◎ Space: development - Applications

All: 11

Requested State	Name	Instances	Disk Quota	Memory	Actions
Started	02RhD86I10w7WQ0Q-wavepress-ui	1/1	Unlimited	512 MB	▷ ⊙ 🗑
Started	api	1/1	Unlimited	1024 MB	▷ ⊙ 🗑
Started	db	1/1	Unlimited	256 MB	▷ ⊙ 🗑
Started	di-builder	1/1	Unlimited	256 MB	▷ ⊙ 🗑
Started	emhHRiCkM4iTBB2TWAVE-X-20-waveapi	1/1	Unlimited	512 MB	▷ ⊙ 🗑
Started	hzooM4A49nLa4RsZ-wavepress-api	1/1	Unlimited	512 MB	▷ ⊙ 🗑
Started	T2ejMOXWtbRrr8ETKWAVE-X-20-waveui	1/1	Unlimited	512 MB	▷ ⊙ 🗑
Started	ui	1/1	Unlimited	1024 MB	▷ ⊙ 🗑
Started	waveapi	1/1	Unlimited	1024 MB	▷ ⊙ 🗑
Stopped	wavedb	0/1	Unlimited	256 MB	▷ ⊙ 🗑
Started	waveui	1/1	Unlimited	1024 MB	▷ ⊙ 🗑

Figure 5-5. *Multiple instances of the Fiori application after being deployed to XSA*

After deploying to the XSA environment, developers and users receive a URL : PORT combination different from the URL : PORT they used during development, differentiating where their application was deployed to. Visiting this new URL will bring them to the application in the targeted environment. Keep in mind that both applications are kept in the Applications page of the cockpit since they are running in parallel and they are deployed to different ports as if they were microservices. This is a very exciting topic that has gained a lot of popularity lately. Check out my book *Microservices in SAP HANA XSA* (Apress, 2020) to learn more about microservices.

Should you want to see how the Fiori application is developed to the SAP Cloud Platform, please proceed with the next few steps. Beware that the same application can be deployed to multiple endpoints; however, developers must ensure that their web applications can reach any OData services that are consuming. Run a few integration validations when you have different domains for your OData service and for your Fiori application. There may be additional steps to perform, for example, creating a Destination in the SAP Cloud Platform to trust the destination URL, enabling CORS (cross-origin resource sharing), or even getting your network team involved to allow the Fiori application to make external domain calls. To create a destination, go to the SAP Cloud Platform Cockpit and select the Destinations menu item from the left navigation list, as shown in Figure 5-6.

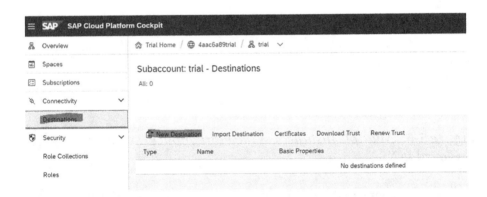

Figure 5-6. *Destinations in SCP*

Then, follow the steps in Figure 5-7 and provide the necessary information to reach and test the destination from the SAP Cloud Platform. The same screen allows SCP admins to set up trusted certificates.

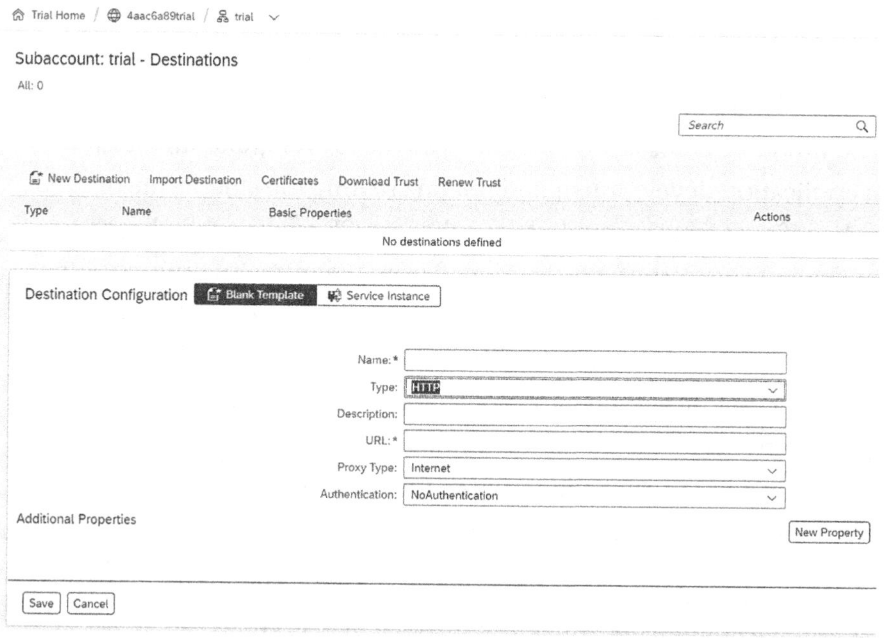

Figure 5-7. *Destination details to create, import destinations or certificates*

To achieve a deployment of the Fiori application into the SAP Cloud Platform, developers must have an account in the platform itself allowing them to create, deploy, and maintain applications, and further, to set up other settings within the cloud environment. The SAP Cloud Platform architecture is based on the CF architecture. The Neo version of the SAP Cloud Platform does not follow these standards. Before showing the steps to deploy the Fiori application to the SCP, make sure to understand and grasp the CF architecture model. In my other book, *Building Microservices in SAP HANA XSA*, https://www.apress.com/us/book/9781484261170, there is more information about CF and about the microservices that can be built using SAP HANA XSA.

CF is an open source cloud application platform. CF is made up of a group of companies such as IBM, SAP, Microsoft, Google, and others, coming together to set up industry standards allowing applications to be runnable across cloud providers so that developers can focus on application development and not on creating the cloud. One of the benefits of creating applications that are CF ready is that these applications are essentially decoupled from the infrastructure, so when they are ready to be moved to on-premise, public, or other private clouds, these applications are easily migrated from one environment/cloud to another. Before getting into applications, it is appropriate to look at CF's hierarchical organization and some important concepts we will be interacting with: organization, space, application, services, and roles, as presented in the screenshot in Figure 5-8.

1) An organization (org) is defined as a development account where one or more developers (known as contributors) with access known as user accounts. These contributors have special roles assigned to them to manage, audit, and build cloud-ready applications or grant access to others. For demonstration purposes, the examples provided in this book will have an organization already created, and it is in an active status. Only an admin can change the status of this org; however, we will assume it is active for the rest of our exercises.

2) Within an organization, there can be one or more spaces. A space is defined as a partition within the org dedicated to building, deploying, and maintaining applications. Every application is scoped to one space. Having an application will eventually require granting roles for access to that application. Application roles belong to one and only one space.

3) Applications and services are the next level within the hierarchy of CF. These applications and services allow users to display and consume data.

4) Users may have one or more roles (role collections are templates) assigned to them. These roles allow the users to develop, access, manage, or audit applications, spaces, or even orgs. Application security is a very complex part of software systems. Security in the cloud (and in HANA XSA) can be its very own extensive topic. There are several other books currently available that explain SAP HANA XSA security in extensive detail. For this book, there will be enough security already implemented to access an OData service from the Fiori application.

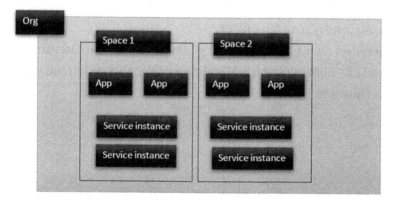

Figure 5-8. *CF hierarchy architecture*

There are different ways to interact with the CF instances. One of them is via the command-line interface (CLI). The CLI can be combined with Linux commands, such as pipe, grep, and others. There are various commands which we will have to interact with the cloud/XSA architecture, such as logging in, setting up services, and creating, editing, building, deploying, or even scaling an application or service. The CF CLI is a versatile tool that allows developers to interact with their cloud instance. It is easy to automate and script other processes that otherwise would require a human to type commands. It minimizes the risk of introducing errors, while interacting with the cloud and keeping it available for developers and admins who would require knowing cloud container details.

Examples of such commands are

```
cf login <USER_NAME>            # to log in to the cloud instance
cf apps | grep <APP_NAME>       # to retrieve an application from
the list of applications
cf push <APP_NAME>              # pushing an application to the
cf instance
cf scale <APP_NAME> -m <MEMORY_SIZE> -i <INTANCES>
```

A comprehensive list of available commands is shown here: http:// cli.cloudfoundry.org/en-US/cf/

Otherwise, once CF CLI is installed on a system, one can run the command cf --help to see how to utilize a command and to see what flags it has, as shown in Figure 5-9.

```
Route and domain management:
  routes,r          delete-route      create-domain
  domains           map-route
  create-route      unmap-route

Space management:
  spaces            create-space      set-space-role
  space-users       delete-space      unset-space-role

Org management:
  orgs,o        set-org-role
  org-users     unset-org-role

CLI plugin management:
  plugins           add-plugin-repo        repo-plugins
  install-plugin    list-plugin-repos

Commands offered by installed plugins:
  bg-deploy                   mta         purge-mta-config
  deploy                      mta-ops     undeploy
  download-mta-op-logs,dmol   mtas

Global options:
  --help, -h                          Show help
  -v                                  Print API request diagnostics to stdout

TIP: Use 'cf help -a' to see all commands.
hxehost:hxeadm>
```

Figure 5-9. *CF CLI*

To deploy our Fiori application to SCP, select the mtar file generated from the workspace project, then select "Deploy to" and select SAP Cloud Platform. As you become aware of the CF architecture, you will need to choose the space to deploy your application to next. If you are running the SAP Cloud trial edition, by default, the SCP already provided an org for you when you enabled your CF mode within the platform. Let us see the steps in the SAP Cloud Platform to retrieve the settings you will need. Go to your SCP account (or register one for free). Once you enter, you will see the screen shown in Figure 5-10.

Figure 5-10. *SAP Cloud Platform trial account*

Then, observe that the SCP uses AWS behind the scenes, as shown in Figure 5-11. The book will go over AWS later at the end of this chapter. It is important to remember the region where these resources are being created.

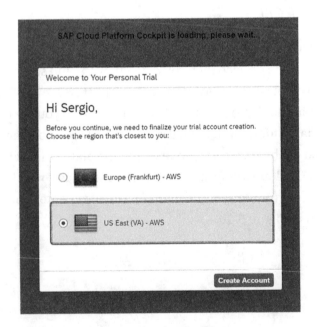

Figure 5-11. *SCP using AWS East (VA) region*

This process, shown in Figure 5-12, may take a few minutes to complete. Once it finishes, you will be able to continue.

Figure 5-12. *Setting up the trial account*

After the account is created, the browser will redirect you to the SCP Cockpit screen shown in Figure 5-13. Take a careful look at the different features in this dashboard so that you can reference it later or even delete the trial account in case you do not use it.

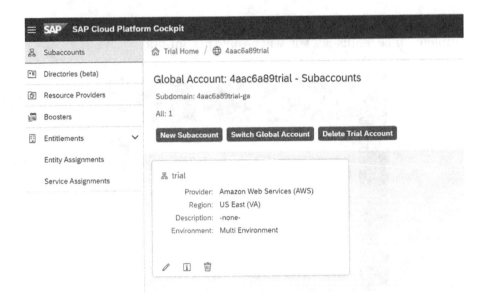

Figure 5-13. *SCP Cockpit showing the global account settings*

Select the tile "trial" global account to proceed to your subaccount.

In the following screen, you can see all the cloud settings that you will need to use for the deployment. The image shown in Figure 5-14 is one of those that should considered as worth a thousand words, since this information is going to be useful for your deployments, for your maintenance, and more importantly for any other future development. Analyze this dashboard and familiarize yourself with this screen in Figure 5-14, and all the important settings related to the CF architecture such as Org Name, Space Name, and the API endpoint, which will be needed on the SAP Web IDE when you decide to deploy from that IDE tool.

Figure 5-14. *SCP CF settings in subaccount trial*

Notice that there is only a single space created; moreover, no applications live in it yet. That number should increase after completing the deployment. If you are doing this exercise in an SCP trial account, you will also see the number of days your cloud instance is enabled for, which is shown on the top right-hand corner of your browser (30 days by default). Should you require additional days to use for your demo, you may request that from SCP. There may be limited features if you are in a trial account, as I will show next. Since you have the Cloud Platform settings described in the previous paragraph, return to your SAP Web IDE and follow the next steps to deploy your application to the SCP environment:

1) Assuming you have already generated an mtar file, select the mtar file you wish to deploy

2) Select the Deploy menu, then select "Deploy to SAP Cloud Platform" as shown in Figure 5-15

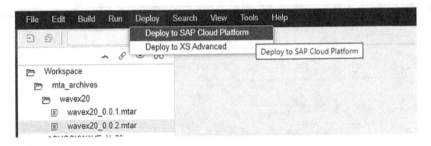

Figure 5-15. *SAP Web IDE deploying to SCP*

In the create sample cloud application in the SCP tutorial, `https://` `developers.sap.com/tutorials/s4sdk-cloud-foundry-sample-` `application.html`, developers can also observe that the following endpoints apply depending on the region selected – your endpoint will show as displayed in Figure 5-16. If it does not show, type one of the following endpoints in the drop-down control.

1) For EU (Europe) use `https://api.cf.eu10.hana.` `ondemand.com` AWS platform

2) For US East (VA) `https://api.cf.us10.hana.` `ondemand.com` AWS platform

3) For US central `https://api.cf.us20.hana.` `ondemand.com` azure platform

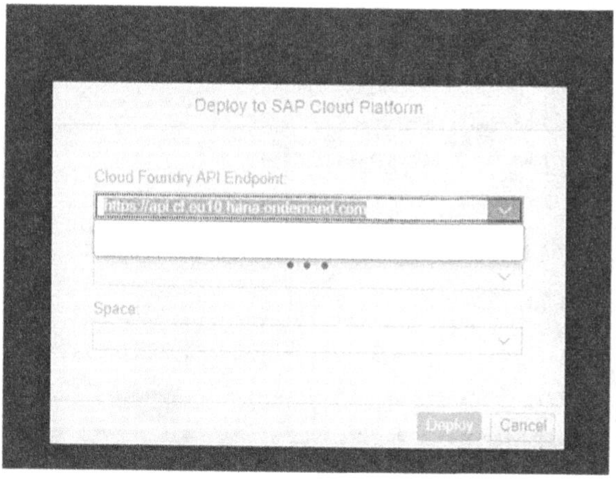

Figure 5-16. *SAP Web IDE showing endpoint on the Cloud Platform*

After selecting the endpoint (which matches your SAP account), enter the account credentials as presented in Figure 5-17.

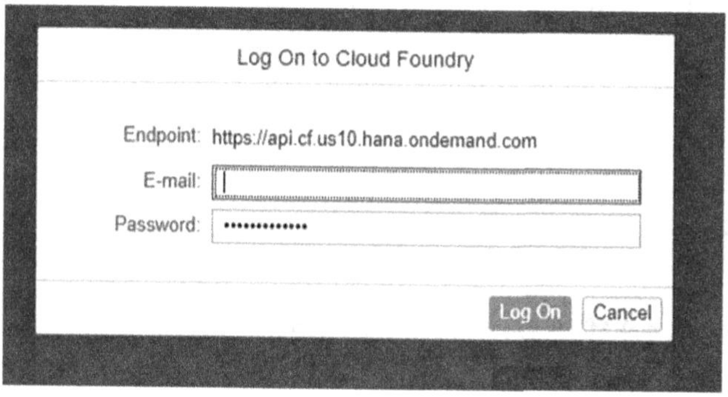

Figure 5-17. *SCP account credentials*

After the SAP Web IDE authenticates you against the SCP, then the next prompt will be presented, so that the deployer selects the organization and a space, as shown in Figure 5-18. Keep in mind that an organization may have one or more spaces. The following exercise only shows the default dev space for illustration purposes – choose a different space if your org has created a different space for your development or your deployments.

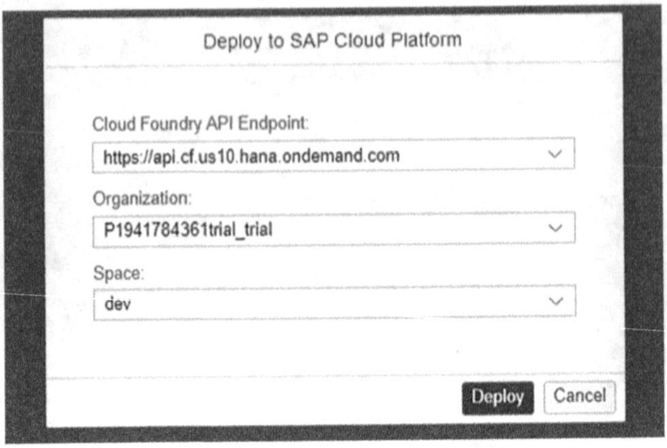

Figure 5-18. SCP cloud hierarchy

In my case, my deployment failed due to a database configuration setting; however, if you are deploying only your custom Fiori application, you should be able to complete the deployment. Look at the console log, as in Figure 5-19, to understand if the deployment was completed or if any settings in your Fiori application need to be edited.

Figure 5-19. SAP Web IDE error during deployment

Deploying to Different Platforms Such as SAP Cloud and AWS

The previous subsection described the steps that developers can follow to build and deploy the Fiori application from the SAP Web IDE into the SAP Cloud Platform. There are other cloud providers that can also be used to host Fiori applications. This section of the chapter will explain how to deploy the same Fiori application to an AWS environment. AWS requires a paid account for an EC2 instance to be able to load the SAP HANA XSA express edition image on top of it.

For this book, I chose AWS, because I am already familiar with this process and I have done this implementation a few times. Believe it or not, every time I run these steps, I learn something new, and it has been no different during the writing of this book. Just like the book explained the CF architecture and hierarchy, I think it is only fair to introduce a few concepts that are used from the AWS Cloud Platform.

AWS offers a huge list of services that are used for companies around the world to run their day-to-day businesses. AWS is an amazing platform from the point of view of a developer, from the point of view of a cloud customer, and from the point of view of the offerings they have. I have been extremely satisfied with the various services I have explored for my own purposes as well as in writing this book.

Selecting a cloud provider can be challenging for organizations because they are trusting part of their infrastructure (and sometimes their data) to the cloud providers; however, if you make a comparison of going to the cloud, you will realize the many benefits of doing so. Among many benefits, here are a few that come to mind:

1) Going global in minutes. You can deploy your infrastructure, software, and other services around the world within a few clicks and be production ready quickly. No need to wait for long days/weeks to get your hardware ordered and delivered as it was in the on-premise days.

2) Zero maintenance of infrastructure and pay only for what you use. Patches or other maintenance are costs that the cloud provider incurs. You (the customer) are only responsible for the computing power and data retrieval while in use.

3) Responsibility "for the cloud" vs. "in the cloud." You (the customer) must be responsible for what you put **in** the cloud, such as securing your application, database, users, and so on. AWS is responsible **for** the cloud, making sure it is up and running, that its managed services are secure, and that there is no mix of your account with other accounts.

4) Keeping track of the expenses incurred by your services via tags. Your cloud account can set alarms for budgeting purposes and also flag each service to let you know what costs are associated with which services you and your customers are using.

Once you have a good understanding of the benefits of the cloud and you are ready to run your applications in this platform, you will find out that you also need to understand additional AWS concepts. Knowledge of the following terms is required when you are setting up certain services and to understand your billing invoice at the end of the month. Pay close attention when setting up your services:

1) **Region** - this is an isolated geographical area in the world with clustered data centers. There are several regions in North America; for example, US East, US West, Canada. It is recommended for customers to select a region nearby to where their customers are in relationship to this area to minimize the impact on performance and network delays on their software. The concept of regionalism has a great impact on how software and cloud services are consumed. You would want to keep your operations as close to you as possible.

2) **Availability Zone** – an AZ is one or more data
centers within the regions. The reason why there are
multiple AZs within a region is to have redundancy
which yields high availability, resulting in fault-
tolerant proof, independent power, independent
cooling, security, and data protection. AZs within
the US East region are us-east-1, us-east-2. Verify
the AZs within the regions where you are deploying
your software.

These concepts are shown at a high level in Figure 5-20.

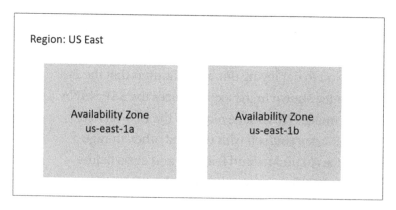

Figure 5-20. *AWS region and AZs*

The next concepts are related to the AWS services. These services must
be deployed to within an AWS region.

1) **Elastic Computing Cloud** - EC2.

This is one of the original and most popular
services, allowing companies to run virtual
computing power. You can think of an EC2 instance
as a virtual machine running within a network in
the cloud. There are various types of EC2 instances

that feature computing power, high memory, and dedicated or spot instances. There are many benefits and features that are set up and available within all these instances, and they are charged on a per-consumption basis.

2) **Elastic Block Store** – EBS

This service features a block storage as one of the methods that allow EC2 instances to store data. There are various services offering storage solutions. Some services are used for large-volume storage, some services are used for persistent storage, and other services are used for memory storage. What you should understand from this service in relation to deploying our application is that the EC2 instance shown in the exercise uses the SAP HANA XSA image. This image requires the EBS service. Familiarize yourself with this and other storage services to understand features and costs before using AWS for your applications.

3) **Simple Storage Service** - S3

This service is one of the most popular AWS services, and it has a high utilization by most cloud customers. A simple storage service is used for object storage such as files, code, backups, and images. The S3 service displays as a folder hierarchy from the AWS UI point of view; however, these objects are stored in a flat hierarchy. This service offers unlimited storage for customers and there are various types of storage depending on the retrieval time required by its consumers. Once again, please familiarize yourself with the different S3 bucket types to decide which one is right for you. In this book's exercises, we will use the S3 service to store and back up our code versioning.

This book will not go into too much depth related to AWS, EC2, EBS, or networking; however, it needs to present a high-level explanation of these managed services for the interest of deploying the custom application into this platform. Should you ever require more in-depth knowledge related to AWS, please consult with an AWS professional. See Figure 5-21 to see how this setup is visualized at a high level.

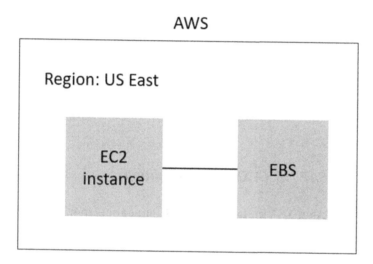

Figure 5-21. *AWS region hosting an EC2 instance connected to an EBS*

For our exercise, we set up the recommended AWS infrastructure as noted in an SAP-provided tutorial: `https://developers.sap.com/ tutorials/hxe-xsa-aws-setup.html`.

The SAP HANA XSA (free) image can be found in the AWS Marketplace, as displayed in Figure 5-22. After selecting the image, you will need to select the region you want to deploy to. The image is a prebuilt instance with some required settings already in place. Using images speeds up the process to get you up and running. Some of the settings already in place for this image are within the security group network rules as well as the volume storage discussed further in the following.

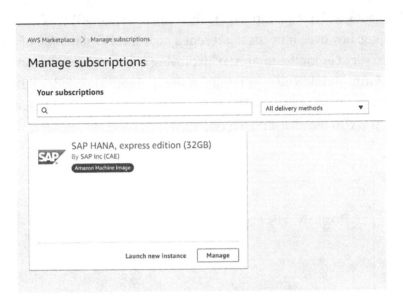

Figure 5-22. *SAP HANA XSA express edition*

This SAP HANA XSA image uses an EC2 instance, m4.2xlarge, which uses EBS storage only, as shown in Figure 5-23.

1. Choose AMI	2. Choose Instance Type	3. Configure Instance	4. Add Storage	5. Add Tags	6. Configure Security Group	7. Review			
Step 2: Choose an Instance Type									
⊘	General purpose	m4.xlarge	4	16	EBS only	Yes	High	Yes	
■	General purpose	m4.2xlarge	8	32	EBS only	Yes	High	Yes	
⊘	General purpose	m4.4xlarge	16	64	EBS only	Yes	High	Yes	
⊘	General purpose	m4.10xlarge	40	160	EBS only	Yes	10 Gigabit	Yes	

Figure 5-23. *SAP HANA XSA - EC2 instance setup*

186

Follow the prompts to set up your XSA environment. Eventually you will need to set up security settings and open some ports to be able to connect to some HANA XSA services and the SAP HANA XSA Web IDE, which will be hosted in AWS; since you used the SAP HANA XSA image, these settings are already in place. You will also need to generate or select an existing key/value pair to connect to your instance using Linux (or Putty if you are using Windows). If you already have a key pair generated, you may be able to use that one. I suggest you create a new one just to have a clean installation of the environment as a whole.

The preceding URL contains all the steps from the SAP official website. If done correctly, it could take 30 mins to 1 hour to complete the setup.

Some of the common errors I encountered when doing the setup were

1) Understanding the difference between Putty and Putty Key Gen

2) Having a basic understanding of using the XS CLI

3) Understanding the reason to use the key pair cert when connecting to your AWS account

4) Generating the ppk file from the pem key. During this step, make sure to select the private key (not public)

5) Understanding the terminal setup steps and making sure you know which commands to use when

Keep in mind that even though the HANA XSA image is free, you still have to pay for the EC2 instance while using it, along with EBS storage. Stopping the EC2 instances does not stop the EBS storage; therefore if you decide to stop your EC2 instance you will still be paying for the EBS service unless you terminate your EC2 instance and EBS volume – you can also learn this the hard way at the end of the month when you receive your bill.

Figure 5-24 shows what it looks like when terminating the EC2 instance and EBS volume. Performing this operation will wipe all your data out, so only proceed with this step when you are completely done with your exercise.

Do not execute this step in a production environment, unless you are completely sure that you want to delete it ALL forever!

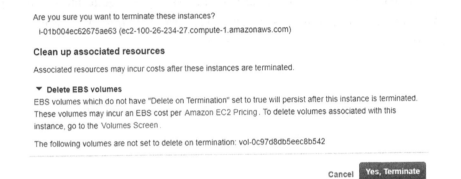

Are you sure you want to terminate these instances?
i-01b004ec62675ae63 (ec2-100-26-234-27.compute-1.amazonaws.com)

Clean up associated resources

Associated resources may incur costs after these instances are terminated.

▼ **Delete EBS volumes**
EBS volumes which do not have "Delete on Termination" set to true will persist after this instance is terminated. These volumes may incur an EBS cost per Amazon EC2 Pricing. To delete volumes associated with this instance, go to the Volumes Screen.

The following volumes are not set to delete on termination: vol-0c97d8db5eec8b542

Cancel   Yes, Terminate

Figure 5-24. *Termination of an EC2 instance and EBS volume*

After setting up the XSA environment in AWS, the easiest way to get your application into that environment is to connect to your GIT account and retrieve the code for your custom Fiori application. See the next few steps on how to connect to GIT, pull the code, and then deploy to the XSA environment using the SAP Web IDE running in AWS.

1) Ensure the SAP Web IDE is up and running. Run the following XS CLI command and notice the status as RUNNING Instances 1/1, as shown in Figure 5-25.

```
hxeadm@hxehost:/usr/sap/HXE/HDB90> xs apps |grep webide
webide                    STARTED           1/1          1.00 GB   <unlimited
>          https://hxehost:53075
hxeadm@hxehost:/usr/sap/HXE/HDB90>
```

Figure 5-25. *Verifying the status of the SAP Web IDE via the XS CLI*

2) Open the browser and navigate to the hxehost:53075 (default port for the webide) and log in as XSA_ ADMIN or XSA_DEV account. Once in the SAP Web IDE, open the settings gear (left navigation icon) and provide the GIT committer your email address and username (they must match the GIT account details), as shown in Figure 5-26.

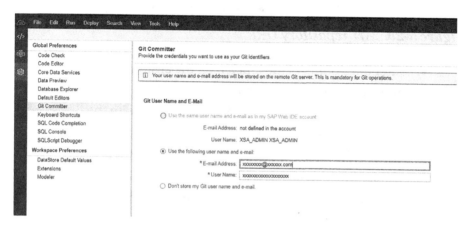

Figure 5-26. *GIT account details*

3) Return to the workspace, right-click it, and select clone repository. When the prompt comes up, provide the URL to clone the GIT repository, as shown in Figures 5-27 and 5-28.

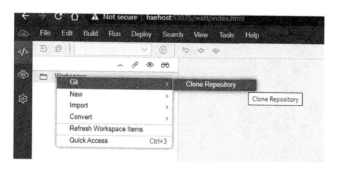

Figure 5-27. *Clone repository*

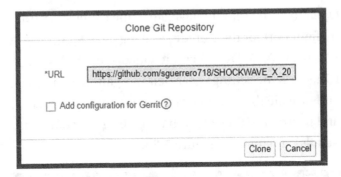

Figure 5-28. *GIT repository URL*

4) After the cloning of the repository, the custom Fiori
    application project will appear in the SAP Web
    IDE. Proceed to build each module, starting with the
    database module, then the api module, and finally
    the ui module. If you are prompted to select a space,
    choose the (default) development space and finally,
    build the project to generate the mtar file as we did
    before, as shown in Figure 5-29.

Keep an eye on the SAP Web IDE console to make sure your modules
and the project build successfully (Figure 5-30). If there are any issues,
then address them before proceeding. You will only be able to deploy if
your project builds successfully.

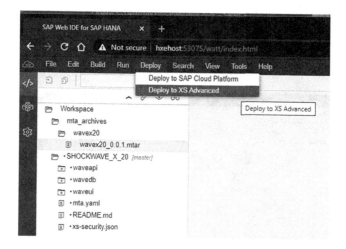

Figure 5-29. *SAP Web IDE generating mtar file in AWS*

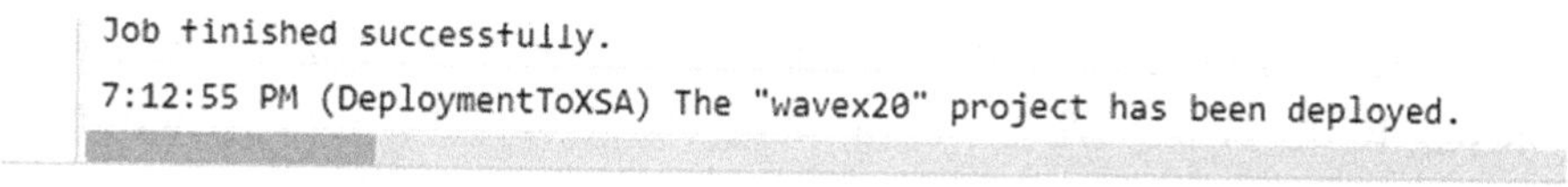

```
Job finished successfully.
7:12:55 PM (DeploymentToXSA) The "wavex20" project has been deployed.
```

Figure 5-30. *Success message after deploying project from the SAP Web IDE*

Open the HANA XS Advanced Cockpit to see the URL where this app was deployed to, as shown in Figure 5-31.

Figure 5-31. *HANA XSA URL for the Fiori application*

191

Then navigate to it from your browser to verify the application truly was deployed (or you may use the Puppeteer script from Chapter 4 to run this step automatically), as shown in Figure 5-32.

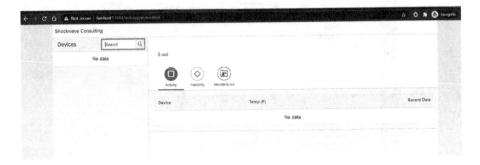

Figure 5-32.   *Custom Fiori application running on AWS*

The screen in Figure 5-32 shows empty list and an empty details page due to the HANA DB not containing any data at the moment since it is a brand-new deployment. However, you can verify that the OData service was indeed called from the custom Fiori application by using the Puppeteer script and editing the URL values, or manually by opening the network tab from the browser and looking at the requests generated, as shown in Figure 5-33.

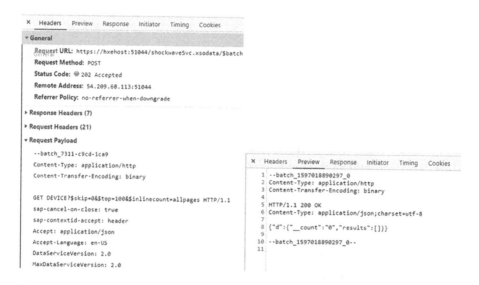

Figure 5-33. *Network tab request headers and response*

Observe that the remote address in Figure 5-33 showing our XSA application is running in the AWS instance.

While this exercise of running the HANA XSA application in AWS seems like an exact exercise from the application being run from the on-premise scenario, this is indeed very close in nature; however, you can tell that running our custom Fiori application in the cloud can be verified from the browser and also using the unit testing scripts from Puppeteer in Chapter 4 of this book.

Moreover, the AWS instance must be running in the EC2 dashboard to be able to run on the browser. A gentle reminder at this point is to remember to stop (or terminate) your EC2 instance when you have completed your development to avoid paying for unnecessary costs in AWS. Keep in mind also that the EBS volume (storage) is running independently from the EC2 instance; therefore, if you wish to terminate your EC2 instance also detach and delete the volume to avoid paying for services you are not using.

GIT Repository

It was briefly mentioned in the subsection about the AWS cloud how the GIT repository can be used to keep development efforts in an external enterprise repository. The reason to use an external repository is to allow the code to be maintained externally to SAP HANA. Furthermore, an external code repository such as GIT is an industry standard that allows teams of developers to work concurrently on their software development using different branching strategies and to keep their deployments clean. There are a few different external repositories; however, the book uses GIT to keep a closer integration with the tools that are provided throughout the exercises of this book.

For simplicity, it is assumed that everyone following the exercises has a valid GIT account and can connect, commit, and clone from a GIT repository using their own license – the book will showcase the use of an account with a free license.

In order to work with GIT, a developer must have access to this repository, be familiar with the GIT commands, and either execute from the command line (if you use this approach you will need to download the GIT CLI) or interact with them from the SAP Web IDE, which already has an interface to a GIT repository. In the previous section, the exercise used the cloning feature to retrieve the code from the GIT repository and used the retrieved code to deploy it to the AWS instance.

The GIT commands are fundamental in the development and maintenance of modern software including SAP Fiori applications, unit testing, and other software development shown here or seen during your day-to-day work. It is required to understand how each of these commands work, and when and how to use them to make yourself more productive when doing your Fiori development. Understanding the commands will also allow you to work with other team members concurrently and it will also allow you to understand code versioning and software deployment and eventually to keep track of new tasks assigned or bug fixes.

Many more commands are available, but not all are shown in Table 5-2. This is a list of the most often used (and not in order):

Table 5-2. *GIT Commands Used from SAP Web IDE*

Command	Description	Example
Clone	Clones the external repository to a local workspace	git clone <url>
Commit	Submits changes from local workspace to the remote repository	git commit -m <comment for commit>
Stash	Saves the changes you do not want to commit immediately	git stash
Push	Pushes your changes to a remote (master) branch	git push <remote> <branch>
Pull	Pulls the changes from the remote branch	git pull <remote> <branch>
Rebase	Process of moving or combining a sequence of commits to a new base commit. The main purpose of a rebase is to maintain project history	git rebase <base>

All these commands can be run from the SAP Web IDE if you select the GIT pane, which is located on the second icon from the top on the right-hand side of your browser screen. Any pending changes will show in the changes table, as shown in Figure 5-34.

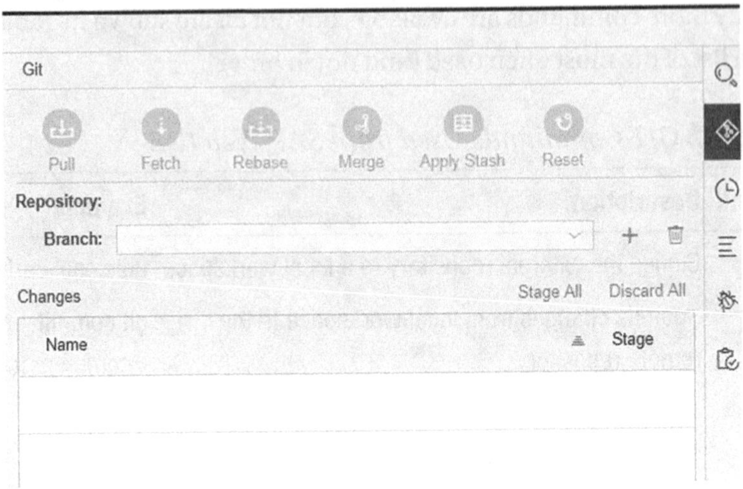

Git

Pull   Fetch   Rebase   Merge   Apply Stash   Reset

Repository:

Branch: [⌄]   +   🗑

Changes   Stage All   Discard All

Name   ⌂   Stage

Figure 5-34. GIT pane in the SAP Web IDE

To save the changes to the repository, a developer must save changes made to the files in the SAP Web IDE, which will show them in the GIT pane with pending changes. Then, the developer must select the file to stage them, enter a comment in the comment input box at the bottom of the GIT pane, and finally select the commit and push button to push these changes into the external repository.

During the different phases of building this custom Fiori application, these steps were executed, and you can see the change logs from the GITHUB repository page, as shown in Figure 5-35 (23 commits, some test commits, some small commits).

⌐ master ▾   ⌐ 1 branch   ◇ 0 tags   Go to file   Add file ▾   ↓ Code ▾

🧑 sguerrero718 detail changes   c43458d 2 days ago   ⓘ 23 commits

Figure 5-35. GITHUB code commits showing in the repository

Whether you are doing custom Fiori development or any other type of software development, chances are that you will interact with an external code repository. Dedicate some time to familiarize yourself with the repository commands. The other external repositories like GITHUB include Bitbucket and MSFT TFS, just to mention two. Both additional external code repositories also work as code repositories for your Fiori development and follow the same commands as the GITHUB repositories when you interact with them. There are plug-ins depending on the tools you are using to interface with these external repositories. Earlier in the book, we also demonstrated the Visual Studio Code editor, which can also interact with GITHUB, Bitbucket, and MSFT TFS.

Automating the Deployment

This is probably going to be the most read section of the book. Everyone wants to make their teams jump on the bandwagon of continuous integration and continuous delivery (CI/CD). What does that mean?

a) Continuous integration is a practice to make frequent commits of code to the repository to make sure the code can "fit in" with the other pieces of the software. Having automated unit testing facilitates the process to run a continuous integration pipeline. If developers make changes to code, deploy, and their software works, then they are following this practice.

b) Continuous delivery relies on continuous integration. Software engineers in charge of deploying developer code must always be able to deploy and have their deployed code to continue to work to ensure delivering new code does not

break existing software systems. Although code
is being integrated constantly, there should not
be a reason why software cannot be delivered in
working condition. It may seem dangerous to run
a continuous delivery pipeline; it takes a lot of
discipline and all hands on board to ensure that the
CI/CD process can run as smoothly as possible, but
it is doable. This type of operation can be achieved
at bigger organizations where there are specialized
teams of engineers facilitating the different moving
pieces.

The ideal situation to have CI/CD in our exercise would require
that all modifications of software be run through an automated unit
testing process, such as the ones shown in Chapter 4. If the automated
test passes all validation, then code is submitted to GITHUB and code
commits are run through a process that verifies software syntax rules, code
coverage, and so on to ensure that it meets a certain set of standards. If
this step is achieved, then the commit could be deployed to the upstream
environment via some tool or script.

Conclusion

As I arrive at the end of the chapter, I am pleased to say that I have enjoyed
being able to deploy this application to different cloud providers. This
chapter started by explaining the versioning of software and provided
some explanation about software releases and what to look for when
maintaining software. After the software versioning, the book explained
and compared the CF architecture and how it is followed from the different
Cloud Platforms including the SAP HANA XSA, which is based on cloud
principles. The steps may be a little different from provider to provider;
however, the concepts between the various platforms follow very similar

steps. After all, the target Cloud Platform is based on the CF architecture. I hope that you can follow the steps and that you can complete your deployment in whatever target platform you choose. There are many tools and approaches to complete your exercise, and this book showed only a few of them.

Closing Thoughts on the Book

As I conclude the writing of the book, I feel extremely glad about the various topics shared throughout the exercises. It seems like a long time ago I was writing about creating custom Fiori applications and starting with a whiteboard design. Shortly after that, I quickly moved into the various floor plans and application types that can be developed for the purpose of Fiori applications. Then, the book introduced various tools to develop, set up, and extend Fiori applications using SAP-provided tools such as the SAP Web IDE, the SAP Web IDE personal edition, and also external IDE tools such as the Visual Studio Code editor with some extensions provided by SAP. After presenting the tools and the development of the Fiori application showing the MVS pattern with XML views, JavaScript controllers, and the various ways to present and model data, the book then made a turn into the unit testing frameworks, which I believe comprise an area that needs to be explored more and more by companies. I concluded the book by explaining the steps required, introducing software versioning, and deploying our developed custom Fiori application to various platforms. I hope you were able to follow along and learn a few tricks from at least some of the chapters, whether you learned something in terms of design, the integration to third-party JavaScript libraries, adding software versioning, or even deploying to the different platforms. Thank you very much for the time you took to follow my journey, and I wish you the best of luck on your custom Fiori development.

APPENDIX A

References

The following sources are references used in writing this book and are also suggested for readers to complement their knowledge while creating custom Fiori applications.

- `https://experience.sap.com/fiori-design-web/` This resource contains the Fiori guidelines.

- `https://developers.sap.com/topics/sap-webide.html` This resource is for learning about the SAP Web IDE tool used for developing Fiori applications.

- `https://www.postman.com/` This tool is used for validations while calling REST APIs (and OData services).

- `https://sapui5.hana.ondemand.com/` This is the SAPUI5 reference library used to create Fiori applications.

- `https://openui5.org/` This is the open source version of the SAPUI5 library.

- `https://help.sap.com/viewer/3504ec5ef1654877861 0c7e89cc0eac3/Cloud/en-US/73beb06e127f4e47b849a a95344aabe1.html` This reference helps you get familiar with the SAP Cloud Platform.

© Sergio Guerrero 2021
S. Guerrero, *Custom Fiori Applications in SAP HANA*,
https://doi.org/10.1007/978-1-4842-6358-7

- `https://tools.hana.ondemand.com/#sapui5` This reference contains the different versions of SAPUI5 for the different IDEs.

- `https://www.odata.org/` This is the official OData site to learn more about OData syntax.

- `https://experience.sap.com/skillup/scenes-new-method-tool-create-storyboards/` This source helps you with the Fiori design.

- `https://aws.amazon.com/ebs/?ebs-whats-new.sort-by=item.additionalFields.postDateTime&ebs-whats-new.sort-order=desc` This source explains the type of storage needed to run the Fiori application in AWS.

- `https://aws.amazon.com/ec2/?nc2=h_ql_prod_fs_ec2` This source explains the computing instance needed to run the HANA XSA environment in AWS.

- `https://aws.amazon.com/s3/?nc2=h_ql_prod_fs_s3` This source explains another storage service in AWS that can be used for backups.

- `https://github.com/` This source is used as an external code repository following industry standards.

- `https://developers.google.com/web/tools/puppeteer` This source explains in detail the Puppeteer unit testing framework.

- `https://qunitjs.com/intro/` This source explains the QUnit framework that comes with SAPUI5, out of the box.

- `http://www.nightmarejs.org/` This source explains the Nightmare JS unit testing framework.

Index

Printed in the United States
By Bookmasters